The Ancient Silk Road

Editor

Libbie Tillery

Scribbles

Year of Publication 2018

ISBN : 9789352979653

Book Published by

Scribbles

(An Imprint of Alpha Editions)

email - alphaedis@gmail.com

Produced by: PediaPress GmbH
Limburg an der Lahn
Germany
http://pediapress.com/

The content within this book was generated collaboratively by volunteers. Please be advised that nothing found here has necessarily been reviewed by people with the expertise required to provide you with complete, accurate or reliable information. Some information in this book may be misleading or simply wrong. Alpha Editions and PediaPress does not guarantee the validity of the information found here. If you need specific advice (for example, medical, legal, financial, or risk management) please seek a professional who is licensed or knowledgeable in that area.

Sources, licenses and contributors of the articles and images are listed in the section entitled "References". Parts of the books may be licensed under the GNU Free Documentation License. A copy of this license is included in the section entitled "GNU Free Documentation License"

The views and characters expressed in the book are those of the contributors and his/her imagination and do not represent the views of the Publisher.

Contents

Articles   **1**

Introduction   **1**
    Silk Road 1

Cities along the Silk Road   **47**
    Cities along the Silk Road 47

Northern Silk Road   **59**
    Northern Silk Road 59

Tea Horse Road   **61**
    Tea Horse Road 61

Maritime Silk Road   **69**
    Maritime Silk Road 69

Appendix   **71**
    References 71
    Article Sources and Contributors 76
    Image Sources, Licenses and Contributors 77

Article Licenses   **79**

Index   **81**

Introduction

Silk Road

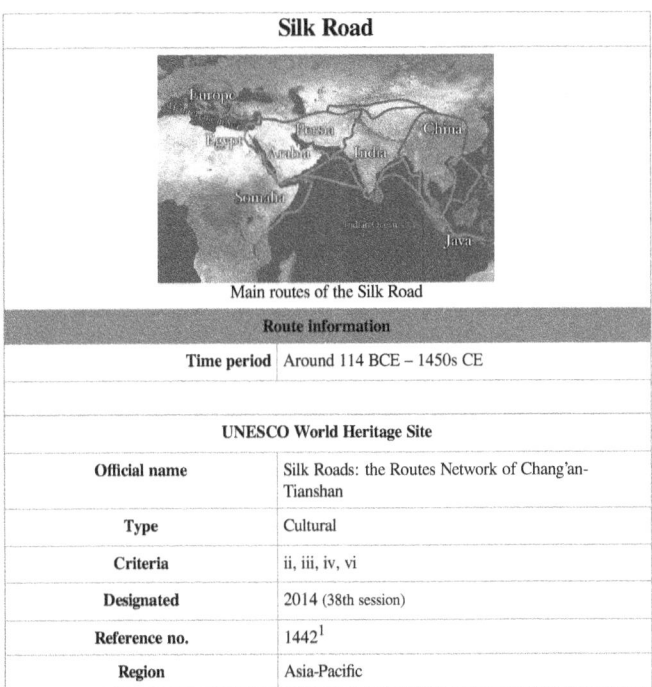

Silk Road	
Main routes of the Silk Road	
Route information	
Time period	Around 114 BCE – 1450s CE
UNESCO World Heritage Site	
Official name	Silk Roads: the Routes Network of Chang'an-Tianshan
Type	Cultural
Criteria	ii, iii, iv, vi
Designated	2014 (38th session)
Reference no.	1442[1]
Region	Asia-Pacific

The **Silk Road** was an ancient network of trade routes that connected the East and West. It was central to cultural interaction between the regions for many centuries. The Silk Road refers to both the terrestrial and the maritime routes

Figure 1: *Woven silk textile from Tomb No. 1 at Mawangdui, Changsha, Hunan province, China, dated to the Western Han Era, 2nd century BCE*

connecting East Asia and Southeast Asia with East Africa, West Asia and Southern Europe.

The Silk Road derives its name from the lucrative trade in silk carried out along its length, beginning in the Han dynasty (207 BCE–220 CE). The Han dynasty expanded the Central Asian section of the trade routes around 114 BCE through the missions and explorations of the Chinese imperial envoy Zhang Qian. The Chinese took great interest in the safety of their trade products and extended the Great Wall of China to ensure the protection of the trade route.[2]

Trade on the Road played a significant role in the development of the civilizations of China, Korea, Japan, India, Iran, Afghanistan, Europe, the Horn of Africa and Arabia, opening long-distance political and economic relations between the civilizations.[3] Though silk was the major trade item exported from China, many other goods were traded, as well as religions, syncretic philosophies, sciences, and technologies. Diseases, most notably plague, also spread along the Silk Road. In addition to economic trade, the Silk Road was a route for cultural trade among the civilizations along its network.[4]

Traders in ancient history included the Bactrians, Sogdians, Syrians, Jews, Arabs, Iranians, Turkmens, Chinese, Malays, Indians, Somalis, Greeks, Romans, Georgians, Armenians, and Azerbaijanis.[5]

In June 2014, UNESCO designated the Chang'an-Tianshan corridor of the Silk Road as a World Heritage Site. The Indian portion is on the tentative site list.

Name

The Silk Road derives its name from the lucrative Asian silk, a major reason for the connection of trade routes into an extensive transcontinental network.[6,7] The German terms *Seidenstraße* and *Seidenstraßen* ("the Silk Road(s)") were coined by Ferdinand von Richthofen, who made seven expeditions to China from 1868 to 1872.[8,9,10] The term Silk Route is also used.[11] Although the term was coined in the 19th century, it did not gain widespread acceptance in academia or popularity among the public until the 20th century. The first book entitled *The Silk Road* was by Swedish geographer Sven Hedin in 1938. The fall of the Soviet Union and 'Iron Curtain' in 1989 led to a surge of public and academic interest in Silk Road sites and studies in the former Soviet republics of Central Asia.

Use of the term 'Silk Road' is not without its detractors. For instance, Warwick Ball contends that the maritime spice trade with India and Arabia was far more consequential for the economy of the Roman Empire than the silk trade with China, which at sea was conducted mostly through India and on land was handled by numerous intermediaries such as the Sogdians.[12] Going as far as to call the whole thing a "myth" of modern academia, Ball argues that there was no coherent overland trade system and no free movement of goods from East Asia to the West until the period of the Mongol Empire.[13] He notes that traditional authors discussing East-West trade such as Marco Polo and Edward Gibbon never labelled any route a "silk" one in particular.

History

Precursors

Chinese and Central Asian contacts

Central Eurasia has been known from ancient times for its horse riding and horse breeding communities, and the overland Steppe Route across the northern steppes of Central Eurasia was in use long before that of the Silk Road. Archeological sites such as the Berel burial ground in Kazakhstan, confirmed that the nomadic Arimaspians were not only breeding horses for trade but also great craftsmen able to propagate exquisite art pieces along the Silk Road. From the 2nd millennium BCE, nephrite jade was being traded from mines in the region of Yarkand and Khotan to China. Significantly, these mines were not very far from the lapis lazuli and spinel ("Balas Ruby") mines in Badakhshan, and, although separated by the formidable Pamir Mountains, routes across them were apparently in use from very early times.Wikipedia:Citation needed

Figure 2: *Chinese jade and steatite plaques, in the Scythian-style animal art of the steppes. 4th–3rd century BCE. British Museum.*

Some remnants of what was probably Chinese silk dating from 1070 BCE have been found in Ancient Egypt. The Great Oasis cities of Central Asia played a crucial role in the effective functioning of the Silk Road trade. The originating source seems sufficiently reliable, but silk degrades very rapidly, so it cannot be verified whether it was cultivated silk (which almost certainly came from China) or a type of *wild silk*, which might have come from the Mediterranean or Middle East.[14]

Following contacts between Metropolitan China and nomadic western border territories in the 8th century BCE, gold was introduced from Central Asia, and Chinese jade carvers began to make imitation designs of the steppes, adopting the Scythian-style animal art of the steppes (depictions of animals locked in combat). This style is particularly reflected in the rectangular belt plaques made of gold and bronze, with other versions in jade and steatite.Wikipedia:Citation needed An elite burial near Stuttgart, Germany, dated to the 6th century BCE, was excavated and found to have not only Greek bronzes but also Chinese silks.[15] Similar animal-shaped pieces of art and wrestler motifs on belts have been found in Scythian grave sites stretching from the Black Sea region all the way to Warring States era archaeological sites in Inner Mongolia (at Aluchaideng) and Shaanxi (at Keshengzhuang) in China.

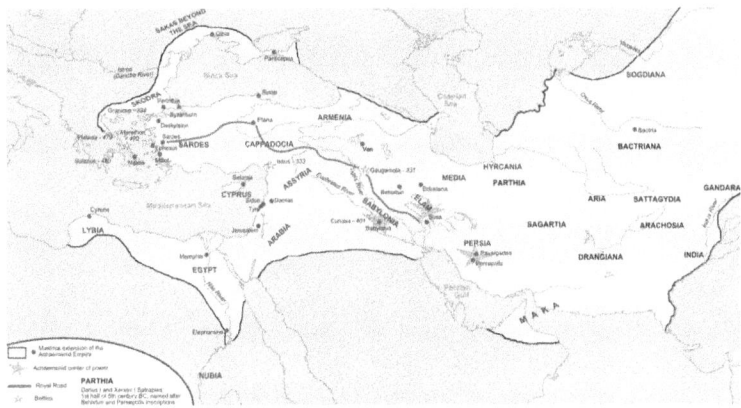

Figure 3: *Achaemenid Persian Empire at its greatest extent, showing the Royal Road.*

The expansion of Scythian cultures, stretching from the Hungarian plain and the Carpathian Mountains to the Chinese Kansu Corridor, and linking the Middle East with Northern India and the Punjab, undoubtedly played an important role in the development of the Silk Road. Scythians accompanied the Assyrian Esarhaddon on his invasion of Egypt, and their distinctive triangular arrowheads have been found as far south as Aswan. These nomadic peoples were dependent upon neighbouring settled populations for a number of important technologies, and in addition to raiding vulnerable settlements for these commodities, they also encouraged long-distance merchants as a source of income through the enforced payment of tariffs. Sogdians played a major role in facilitating trade between China and Central Asia along the Silk Roads as late as the 10th century, their language serving as a *lingua franca* for Asian trade as far back as the 4th century.[16,17]

Persian Royal Road

By the time of Herodotus (c. 475 BCE), the Royal Road of the Persian Empire ran some 2,857 km (1,775 mi) from the city of Susa on the Karun (250 km (155 mi) east of the Tigris) to the port of Smyrna (modern İzmir in Turkey) on the Aegean Sea.[18] It was maintained and protected by the Achaemenid Empire (c. 500–330 BCE) and had postal stations and relays at regular intervals. By having fresh horses and riders ready at each relay, royal couriers could carry messages and traverse the length of the road in nine days, while normal travellers took about three months.Wikipedia:Citation needed

Figure 4: *Probable Greek soldier with a Greek mythological centaur in the Sampul tapestry,*[19] *woollen wall hanging, 3rd–2nd century BCE, Sampul, Urumqi Xinjiang Museum, China.*

Hellenistic era

The next major step in the development of the Silk Road was the expansion of the Greek empire of Alexander the Great into Central Asia. In August 329 BC, at the mouth of the Fergana Valley in Tajikistan, he founded the city of Alexandria Eschate or "Alexandria The Furthest".[20]

The Greeks remained in Central Asia for the next three centuries, first through the administration of the Seleucid Empire, and then with the establishment of the Greco-Bactrian Kingdom (250–125 BCE) in Bactria (modern Afghanistan, Tajikistan, and Pakistan) and the later Indo-Greek Kingdom (180 BCE – 10 CE) in modern Northern Pakistan and Afghanistan. They continued to expand eastward, especially during the reign of Euthydemus (230–200 BCE), who extended his control beyond Alexandria Eschate to Sogdiana. There are indications that he may have led expeditions as far as Kashgar in Chinese Turkestan, leading to the first known contacts between China and the West around 200 BCE. The Greek historian Strabo writes, *"they extended their empire even as far as the Seres (China) and the Phryni."*

The Hellenistic world and Classical Greek philosophy mixed with Eastern philosophies,[21] leading to syncretisms such as Greco-Buddhism.

Chinese exploration of Central Asia

With the Mediterranean linked to the Fergana Valley, the next step was to open a route across the Tarim Basin and the Hexi Corridor to China Proper. This extension came around 130 BCE, with the embassies of the Han dynasty to Central Asia following the reports of the ambassador Zhang Qian (who was originally sent to obtain an alliance with the Yuezhi against the Xiongnu). Zhang Qian visited directly the kingdom of Dayuan in Ferghana, the territories of the Yuezhi in Transoxiana, the Bactrian country of Daxia with its remnants of Greco-Bactrian rule, and Kangju. He also made reports on neighbouring countries that he did not visit, such as Anxi (Parthia), Tiaozhi (Mesopotamia), Shendu (Pakistan) and the Wusun. Zhang Qian's report suggested the economic reason for Chinese expansion and wall-building westward, and trailblazed the silk road, which is one of the most famous trade routes. After the defeat of the Xiongnu, however, Chinese armies established themselves in Central Asia, initiating the Silk Route as a major avenue of international trade. Some say that the Chinese Emperor Wu became interested in developing commercial relationships with the sophisticated urban civilizations of Ferghana, Bactria, and the Parthian Empire: "The Son of Heaven on hearing all this reasoned thus: Ferghana (Dayuan *"Great Ionians"*) and the possessions of Bactria (Ta-Hsia) and Parthian Empire (Anxi) are large countries, full of rare things, with a population living in fixed abodes and given to occupations somewhat identical with those of the Chinese people, but with weak armies, and placing great value on the rich produce of China" (*Hou Hanshu*, Later Han History). Others[22] say that Emperor Wu was mainly interested in fighting the Xiongnu and that major trade began only after the Chinese pacified the Hexi Corridor.

The Silk Roads' origin lay in the hands of the Chinese. The soil in China lacked Selenium, a deficiency which contributed to muscular weakness and reduced growth in horses. Consequently, horses in China were too frail to support the weight of a Chinese soldier. The Chinese needed the superior horses that nomads bred on the Eurasian steppes, and nomads wanted things only agricultural societies produced, such as grain and silk. Even after the construction of the Great Wall, nomads gathered at the gates of the wall to exchange. Soldiers sent to guard the wall were often paid in silk which they traded with the nomads. Past its inception, the Chinese continued to dominate the Silk Roads, a process which was accelerated when "China snatched control of the Silk Road from the Hsiung-nu" and the Chinese general Cheng Ki "installed himself as protector of the Tarim at Wu-lei, situated between Kara Shahr and Kucha." "China's control of the Silk Road at the time of the later Han, by ensuring the freedom of transcontinental trade along the double chain of oases north and

Figure 5: *A ceramic horse head and neck (broken from the body), from the Chinese Eastern Han dynasty (1st–2nd century CE)*

Figure 6: *Bronze coin of Constantius II (337–361), found in Karghalik, Xinjiang, China*

south of the Tarim, favoured the dissemination of Buddhism in the river basin, and with it Indian literature and Hellenistic art." The Chinese were also strongly attracted by the tall and powerful horses (named "Heavenly horses") in the possession of the Dayuan (literally the "Great Ionians", the Greek kingdoms of Central Asia), which were of capital importance in fighting the nomadic Xiongnu. The Chinese subsequently sent numerous embassies, around ten every year, to these countries and as far as Seleucid Syria. "Thus more embassies were dispatched to Anxi [Parthia], Yancai [who later joined the Alans], Lijian [Syria under the Greek Seleucids], Tiaozhi (Mesopotamia), and Tianzhu [northwestern India]... As a rule, rather more than ten such missions went forward in the course of a year, and at the least five or six." (*Hou Hanshu*, Later Han History).These connections marked the beginning of the Silk Road trade network that extended to the Roman Empire.[23] The Chinese campaigned in Central Asia on several occasions, and direct encounters between Han troops and Roman legionaries (probably captured or recruited as mercenaries by the Xiong Nu) are recorded, particularly in the 36 BCE battle of Sogdiana (Joseph Needham, Sidney Shapiro). It has been suggested that the Chinese crossbow was transmitted to the Roman world on such occasions, although the Greek gastraphetes provides an alternative origin. R. Ernest Dupuy and Trevor N. Dupuy suggest that in 36 BCE, a "Han expedition into central Asia, west of Jaxartes River, apparently encountered and defeated a contingent of Roman legionaries. The Romans may have been part of Antony's army invading Parthia. Sogdiana (modern Bukhara), east of the Oxus River, on the Polytimetus River, was apparently the most easterly penetration ever made by Roman forces in Asia. The margin of Chinese victory appears to have been their crossbows, whose bolts and darts seem easily to have penetrated Roman shields and armour."[24] The Roman historian Florus also describes the visit of numerous envoys, which included *Seres*(China), to the first Roman Emperor Augustus, who reigned between 27 BCE and 14 CE:

<templatestyles src="Template:Quote/styles.css"/>

Even the rest of the nations of the world which were not subject to the imperial sway were sensible of its grandeur, and looked with reverence to the Roman people, the great conqueror of nations. Thus even Scythians and Sarmatians sent envoys to seek the friendship of Rome. Nay, the Seres came likewise, and the Indians who dwelt beneath the vertical sun, bringing presents of precious stones and pearls and elephants, but thinking all of less moment than the vastness of the journey which they had undertaken, and which they said had occupied four years. In truth it needed but to look at their complexion to see that they were people of another world than ours.

—Henry Yule, Cathay and the Way Thither (1866)

The Han army regularly policed the trade route against nomadic bandit forces generally identified as Xiongnu. Han general Ban Chao led an army of 70,000 mounted infantry and light cavalry troops in the 1st century CE to secure the trade routes, reaching far west to the Tarim basin. Ban Chao expanded his conquests across the Pamirs to the shores of the Caspian Sea and the borders of Parthia.[25] It was from here that the Han general dispatched envoy Gan Ying to Daqin (Rome).[26] The Silk Road essentially came into being from the 1st century BCE, following these efforts by China to consolidate a road to the Western world and India, both through direct settlements in the area of the Tarim Basin and diplomatic relations with the countries of the Dayuan, Parthians and Bactrians further west. The Silk Roads were a "complex network of trade routes" that gave people the chance to exchange goods and culture.[27]

A maritime Silk Route opened up between Chinese-controlled Giao Chỉ (centred in modern Vietnam, near Hanoi), probably by the 1st century. It extended, via ports on the coasts of India and Sri Lanka, all the way to Roman-controlled ports in Roman Egypt and the Nabataean territories on the northeastern coast of the Red Sea. The earliest Roman glassware bowl found in China was unearthed from a Western Han tomb in Guangzhou, dated to the early 1st century BCE, indicating that Roman commercial items were being imported through the South China Sea.[28] According to Chinese dynastic histories, it is from this region that the Roman embassies arrived in China, beginning in 166 CE during the reigns of Marcus Aurelius and Emperor Huan of Han.[29,30] Other Roman glasswares have been found in Eastern-Han-era tombs (25–220 CE) more further inland in Nanjing and Luoyang.[31] P.O. Harper asserts that a 2nd or 3rd-century Roman gilt silver plate found in Jingyuan, Gansu, China with a central image of the Greco-Roman god Dionysus resting on a feline creature, most likely came via Greater Iran (i.e. Sogdiana).[32] Valerie Hansen (2012) believed that earliest Roman coins found in China date to the 4th century, during Late Antiquity and the Dominate period, and come from the Byzantine Empire.[33] However, Warwick Ball (2016) highlights the recent discovery of sixteen Principate-era Roman coins found in Xi'an (formerly Chang'an, one of the two Han capitals) that were minted during the reigns of Roman emperors spanning from Tiberius to Aurelian (i.e. 1st to 3rd centuries CE).[34] It is true that these coins were found in China, but they were deposited there in the twentieth century, not in ancient times, and therefore they do not shed light on historic contacts between China and Rome.[35] Roman golden medallions made during the reign of Antoninus Pius and quite possibly his successor Marcus Aurelius have been found at Óc Eo in southern Vietnam, which was then part of the Kingdom of Funan bordering the Chinese province of Jiaozhi in northern Vietnam.[36,37] Given the archaeological finds of Mediterranean artefacts made

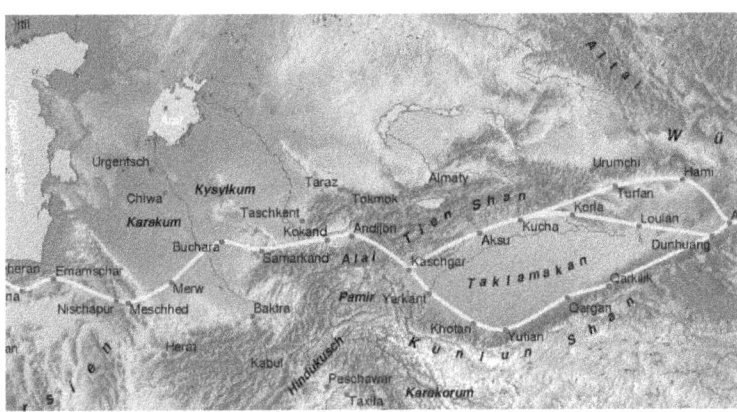

Figure 7: *Central Asia during Roman times, with the first Silk Road*

by Louis Malleret in the 1940s, Óc Eo may have been the same site as the port city of Kattigara described by Ptolemy in his *Geography* (c. 150 CE), although Ferdinand von Richthofen had previously believed it was closer to Hanoi.[38]

Roman Empire

Soon after the Roman conquest of Egypt in 30 BCE, regular communications and trade between China, Southeast Asia, India, the Middle East, Africa, and Europe blossomed on an unprecedented scale. The Roman Empire inherited eastern trade routes that were part of the Silk Road from the earlier Hellenistic powers and the Arabs. With control of these trade routes, citizens of the Roman Empire received new luxuries and greater prosperity for the Empire as a whole.[39] The Roman-style glassware discovered in the archeological sites of Gyeongju, capital of the Silla kingdom (Korea) showed that Roman artifacts were traded as far as the Korean peninsula. The Greco-Roman trade with India started by Eudoxus of Cyzicus in 130 BCE continued to increase, and according to Strabo (II.5.12), by the time of Augustus, up to 120 ships were setting sail every year from Myos Hormos in Roman Egypt to India.[40] The Roman Empire connected with the Central Asian Silk Road through their ports in Barygaza (known today as Bharuch[41]) and Barbaricum (known today as the cities of Karachi, Sindh, and Pakistan[42]) and continued along the western coast of India.[43] An ancient "travel guide" to this Indian Ocean trade route was the Greek Periplus of the Erythraean Sea written in 60 CE.

The travelling party of Maës Titianus penetrated farthest east along the Silk Road from the Mediterranean world, probably with the aim of regularising contacts and reducing the role of middlemen, during one of the lulls in Rome's

Figure 8: *A Westerner on a camel, Northern Wei dynasty (386–534)*

intermittent wars with Parthia, which repeatedly obstructed movement along the Silk Road. Intercontinental trade and communication became regular, organised, and protected by the 'Great Powers.' Intense trade with the Roman Empire soon followed, confirmed by the Roman craze for Chinese silk (supplied through the Parthians), even though the Romans thought silk was obtained from trees. This belief was affirmed by Seneca the Younger in his Phaedra and by Virgil in his Georgics. Notably, Pliny the Elder knew better. Speaking of the *bombyx* or silk moth, he wrote in his Natural Histories "They weave webs, like spiders, that become a luxurious clothing material for women, called silk."[44] The Romans traded spices, glassware, perfumes, and silk.[45]

Roman artisans began to replace yarn with valuable plain silk cloths from China and the Silla Kingdom in Gyeongju, Korea.[46] Chinese wealth grew as they delivered silk and other luxury goods to the Roman Empire, whose wealthy women admired their beauty.[47] The Roman Senate issued, in vain, several edicts to prohibit the wearing of silk, on economic and moral grounds: the import of Chinese silk caused a huge outflow of gold, and silk clothes were considered decadent and immoral. <templatestyles src="Template:Quote/styles.css"/>

> *I can see clothes of silk, if materials that do not hide the body, nor even one's decency, can be called clothes... Wretched flocks of maids labour so that the adulteress may be visible through her thin dress, so that her*

husband has no more acquaintance than any outsider or foreigner with his wife's body.[48]

The West Roman Empire, and its demand for sophisticated Asian products, crumbled in the West around the 5th century.

The unification of Central Asia and Northern India within the Kushan Empire in the 1st to 3rd centuries reinforced the role of the powerful merchants from Bactria and Taxila.[49] They fostered multi-cultural interaction as indicated by their 2nd century treasure hoards filled with products from the Greco-Roman world, China, and India, such as in the archeological site of Begram.

Byzantine Empire

Byzantine Greek historian Procopius stated that two Nestorian Christian monks eventually uncovered the way silk was made. From this revelation, monks were sent by the Byzantine Emperor Justinian (ruled 527–565) as spies on the Silk Road from Constantinople to China and back to steal the silkworm eggs, resulting in silk production in the Mediterranean, particularly in Thrace in northern Greece,[50] and giving the Byzantine Empire a monopoly on silk production in medieval Europe. In 568 the Byzantine ruler Justin II was greeted by a Sogdian embassy representing Istämi, ruler of the Turkic Khaganate, who formed an alliance with the Byzantines against Khosrow I of the Sasanian Empire that allowed the Byzantines to bypass the Sasanian merchants and trade directly with the Sogdians for purchasing Chinese silk.[51,52,53] Although the Byzantines had already procured silkworm eggs from China by this point, the quality of Chinese silk was still far greater than anything produced in the West, a fact that is perhaps emphasized by the discovery of coins minted by Justin II found in a Chinese tomb of Shanxi province dated to the Sui dynasty (581–618).[54]

Both the *Old Book of Tang* and *New Book of Tang*, covering the history of the Chinese Tang dynasty (618–907), record that a new state called *Fu-lin* (拂菻 ; i.e. Byzantine Empire) was virtually identical to the previous *Daqin* (大秦 ; i.e. Roman Empire). Several *Fu-lin* embassies were recorded for the Tang period, starting in 643 with an alleged embassy by Constans II (transliterated as *Bo duo li*, 波多力 , from his nickname "Kōnstantinos Pogonatos") to the court of Emperor Taizong of Tang. The *History of Song* describes the final embassy and its arrival in 1081, apparently sent by Michael VII Doukas (transliterated as *Mie li sha ling kai sa*, 滅力沙靈改撒 , from his name and title Michael VII Parapinakēs Caesar) to the court of Emperor Shenzong of the Song dynasty (960–1279). However, the *History of Yuan* claims that a Byzantine man became a leading astronomer and physician in Khanbaliq, at the court of Kublai Khan, Mongol founder of the Yuan dynasty (1271–1368)

Figure 9: *Coin of Constans II (r. 641–648), who is named in Chinese sources as the first of several Byzantine emperors to send embassies to the Chinese Tang dynasty*

and was even granted the noble title 'Prince of Fu lin' (Chinese: 拂菻王 ; Fú lǐn wáng).[55] The Uyghur Nestorian Christian diplomat Rabban Bar Sauma, who set out from his Chinese home in Khanbaliq (Beijing) and acted as a representative for Arghun (a grandnephew of Kublai Khan),[56,57,58,59] traveled throughout Europe and attempted to secure military alliances with Edward I of England, Philip IV of France, Pope Nicholas IV, as well as the Byzantine ruler Andronikos II Palaiologos.[60] Andronikos II had two half-sisters who were married to great-grandsons of Genghis Khan, which made him an in-law with the Yuan-dynasty Mongol ruler in Beijing, Kublai Khan.[61] The *History of Ming* preserves an account where the Hongwu Emperor, after founding the Ming dynasty (1368–1644), had a supposed Byzantine merchant named Nieh-ku-lun (捏古倫) deliver his proclamation about the establishment of a new dynasty to the Byzantine court of John V Palaiologos in September 1371.[62] Friedrich Hirth (1885), Emil Bretschneider (1888), and more recently Edward Luttwak (2009) presumed that this was none other than Nicolaus de Bentra, a Roman Catholic bishop of Khanbilaq chosen by Pope John XXII to replace the previous archbishop John of Montecorvino.[63]

Figure 10: *A Chinese sancai statue of a Sogdian man with a wineskin, Tang dynasty (618–907)*

Tang dynasty reopens the route

Although the Silk Road was initially formulated during the reign of Emperor Wu of Han (141–87 BCE), it was reopened by the Tang Empire in 639 when Hou Junji conquered the Western Regions, and remained open for almost four decades. It was closed after the Tibetans captured it in 678, but in 699, during Empress Wu's period, the Silk Road reopened when the Tang reconquered the Four Garrisons of Anxi originally installed in 640, once again connecting China directly to the West for land-based trade. The Tang captured the vital route through the Gilgit Valley from Tibet in 722, lost it to the Tibetans in 737, and regained it under the command of the Goguryeo-Korean General Gao Xianzhi.

While the Turks were settled in the Ordos region (former territory of the Xiongnu), the Tang government took on the military policy of dominating the central steppe. The Tang dynasty (along with Turkic allies) conquered and subdued Central Asia during the 640s and 650s. During Emperor Taizong's reign alone, large campaigns were launched against not only the Göktürks, but also separate campaigns against the Tuyuhun, the oasis states, and the Xueyantuo. Under Emperor Taizong, Tang general Li Jing conquered the Eastern Turkic Khaganate. Under Emperor Gaozong, Tang general Su Dingfang conquered

Figure 11: *Caravan on the Silk Road, 1380*

the Western Turkic Khaganate, which was an important ally of Byzantine empire. After these conquests, the Tang dynasty fully controlled the Xiyu, which was the strategic location astride the Silk Road. This led the Tang dynasty to reopen the Silk Road.

The Tang dynasty established a second Pax Sinica, and the Silk Road reached its golden age, whereby Persian and Sogdian merchants benefited from the commerce between East and West. At the same time, the Chinese empire welcomed foreign cultures, making it very cosmopolitan in its urban centres. In addition to the land route, the Tang dynasty also developed the maritime Silk Route. Chinese envoys had been sailing through the Indian Ocean to India since perhaps the 2nd century BCE, yet it was during the Tang dynasty that a strong Chinese maritime presence could be found in the Persian Gulf and Red Sea into Persia, Mesopotamia (sailing up the Euphrates River in modern-day Iraq), Arabia, Egypt, Aksum (Ethiopia), and Somalia in the Horn of Africa.

Post-classical history

The Silk Road represents an early phenomenon of political and cultural integration due to inter-regional trade. In its heyday, it sustained an international culture that strung together groups as diverse as the Magyars, Armenians, and Chinese. The Silk Road reached its peak in the west during the time of the Byzantine Empire; in the Nile-Oxus section, from the Sassanid Empire period to the Il Khanate period; and in the sinitic zone from the Three Kingdoms

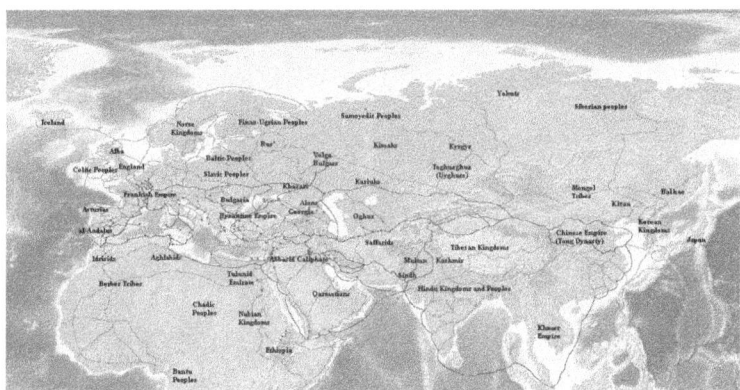

Figure 12: *Map of Eurasia and Africa showing trade networks, c. 870*

period to the Yuan dynasty period. Trade between East and West also developed across the Indian Ocean, between Alexandria in Egypt and Guangzhou in China. Persian Sassanid coins emerged as a means of currency, just as valuable as silk yarn and textiles.[64]

Under its strong integrating dynamics on the one hand and the impacts of change it transmitted on the other, tribal societies previously living in isolation along the Silk Road, and pastoralists who were of barbarian cultural development, were drawn to the riches and opportunities of the civilisations connected by the routes, taking on the trades of marauders or mercenaries.Wikipedia:Citation needed "Many barbarian tribes became skilled warriors able to conquer rich cities and fertile lands and to forge strong military empires."

The Sogdians dominated the East-West trade after the 4th century up to the 8th century, with Suyab and Talas ranking among their main centres in the north. They were the main caravan merchants of Central Asia. Their commercial interests were protected by the resurgent military power of the Göktürks, whose empire has been described as "the joint enterprise of the Ashina clan and the Soghdians".[65] A.V. Dybo noted that "according to historians, the main driving force of the Great Silk Road were not just Sogdians, but the carriers of a mixed Sogdian-Türkic culture that often came from mixed families."[66] Their trade, with some interruptions, continued in the 9th century within the framework of the Uighur Empire, which until 840 extended across northern Central Asia and obtained from China enormous deliveries of silk in exchange for horses. At this time caravans of Sogdians travelling to Upper Mongolia are mentioned in Chinese sources. They played an equally important religious and cultural role. Part of the data about eastern Asia provided by Muslim geographers of

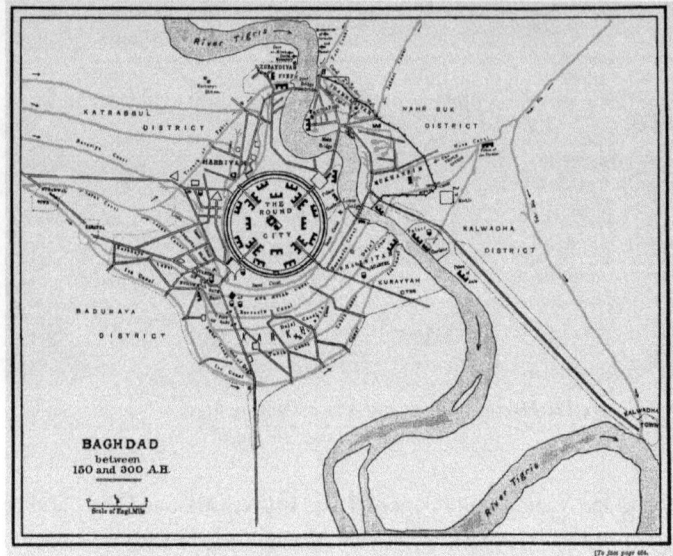

Figure 13: *The Round city of Baghdad between 767 and 912 was the most important urban node along the Silk Road.*

the 10th century actually goes back to Sogdian data of the period 750–840 and thus shows the survival of links between east and west. However, after the end of the Uighur Empire, Sogdian trade went through a crisis. What mainly issued from Muslim Central Asia was the trade of the Samanids, which resumed the northwestern road leading to the Khazars and the Urals and the northeastern one toward the nearby Turkic tribes.

The Silk Road gave rise to the clusters of military states of nomadic origins in North China, ushered the Nestorian, Manichaean, Buddhist, and later Islamic religions into Central Asia and China.

Islamic era and the Silk Road

By the Umayyad era, Damascus had overtaken Ctesiphon as a major trade center until the Abbasid dynasty built the city of Baghdad, which became the most important city along the silk road.

At the end of its glory, the routes brought about the largest continental empire ever, the Mongol Empire, with its political centres strung along the Silk Road (Beijing in North China, Karakorum in central Mongolia, Sarmakhand in Transoxiana, Tabriz in Northern Iran, Sarai and Astrakhan in lower Volga,

Figure 14: *A lion motif on Sogdian polychrome silk, 8th century, most likely from Bukhara*

Solkhat in Crimea, Kazan in Central Russia, Erzurum in eastern Anatolia), realising the political unification of zones previously loosely and intermittently connected by material and cultural goods.Wikipedia:Citation needed

The Islamic world was expanded into Central Asia during the 8th century, under the Umayyad Caliphate, while its successor the Abbasid Caliphate put a halt to Chinese westward expansion at the Battle of Talas in 751 (near the Talas River in modern-day Kyrgyzstan).[67] However, following the disastrous An Lushan Rebellion (755–763) and the conquest of the Western Regions by the Tibetan Empire, the Tang Empire was unable to reassert its control over Central Asia.[68] Contemporary Tang authors noted how the dynasty had gone into decline after this point.[69] In 848 the Tang Chinese, led by the commander Zhang Yichao, were only able to reclaim the Hexi Corridor and Dunhuang in Gansu from the Tibetans.[70] The Persian Samanid Empire (819–999) centered in Bukhara (Uzbekistan) continued the trade legacy of the Sogdians. The disruptions of trade were curtailed in that part of the world by the end of the 10th century and conquests of Central Asia by the Turkic Islamic Kara-Khanid Khanate, yet Nestorian Christianity, Zoroastrianism, Manichaeism, and Buddhism in Central Asia virtually disappeared.[71]

During the early 13th century Khwarezmia was invaded by the early Mongol Empire. The Mongol ruler Genghis Khan had the once vibrant cities of

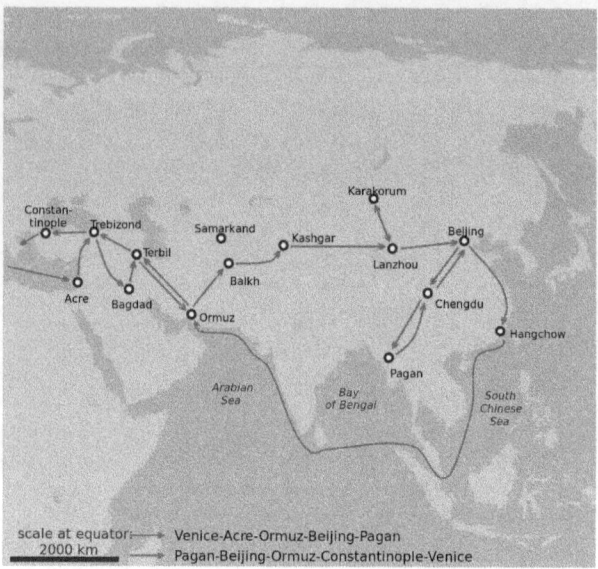

Figure 15: *Map of Marco Polo's travels in 1271–1295*

Bukhara and Samarkand burned to the ground after besieging them.[72] However, in 1370 Samarkand saw a revival as the capital of the new Timurid Empire. The Turko-Mongol ruler Timur forcefully moved artisans and intellectuals from across Asia to Samarkand, making it one of the most important trade centers and cultural *entrepôts* of the Islamic world.[73]

Mongol age

The Mongol expansion throughout the Asian continent from around 1207 to 1360 helped bring political stability and re-established the Silk Road (via Karakorum). It also brought an end to the dominance of the Islamic Caliphate over world trade. Because the Mongols came to control the trade routes, trade circulated throughout the region, though they never abandoned their nomadic lifestyle.

The Mongol rulers wanted to establish their capital on the Central Asian steppe, so to accomplish this goal, after every conquest they enlisted local people (traders, scholars, artisans) to help them construct and manage their empire.[74]

The Mongol diplomat Rabban Bar Sauma visited the courts of Europe in 1287–88 and provided a detailed written report to the Mongols. Around the same time, the Venetian explorer Marco Polo became one of the first Europeans to travel the Silk Road to China. His tales, documented in *The Travels of Marco Polo*, opened Western eyes to some of the customs of the Far East. He was not the first to bring back stories, but he was one of the most widely read. He had been preceded by numerous Christian missionaries to the East, such as William of Rubruck, Benedykt Polak, Giovanni da Pian del Carpine, and Andrew of Longjumeau. Later envoys included Odoric of Pordenone, Giovanni de' Marignolli, John of Montecorvino, Niccolò de' Conti, and Ibn Battuta, a Moroccan Muslim traveller who passed through the present-day Middle East and across the Silk Road from Tabriz between 1325–54.[75]

In the 13th century efforts were made at forming a Franco-Mongol alliance, with an exchange of ambassadors and (failed) attempts at military collaboration in the Holy Land during the later Crusades. Eventually the Mongols in the Ilkhanate, after they had destroyed the Abbasid and Ayyubid dynasties, converted to Islam and signed the 1323 Treaty of Aleppo with the surviving Muslim power, the Egyptian Mamluks.Wikipedia:Citation needed

Some studies indicate that the Black Death, which devastated Europe starting in the late 1340s, may have reached Europe from Central Asia (or China) along the trade routes of the Mongol Empire.[76] One theory holds that Genoese traders coming from the entrepot of Trebizond in northern Turkey carried the disease to Western Europe; like many other outbreaks of plague, there is strong evidence that it originated in marmots in Central Asia and was carried westwards to the Black Sea by Silk Road traders.[77]

Decline and disintegration

The fragmentation of the Mongol Empire loosened the political, cultural, and economic unity of the Silk Road. Turkmeni marching lords seized land around the western part of the Silk Road from the decaying Byzantine Empire. After the fall of the Mongol Empire, the great political powers along the Silk Road became economically and culturally separated. Accompanying the crystallisation of regional states was the decline of nomad power, partly due to the devastation of the Black Death and partly due to the encroachment of sedentary civilisations equipped with gunpowder.

The consolidation of the Ottoman and Safavid empires in the West Asia led to a revival of overland trade, interrupted sporadically by warfare between them. The silk trade continued to flourish until it was disrupted by the collapse of the Safavid Empire in the 1720s.

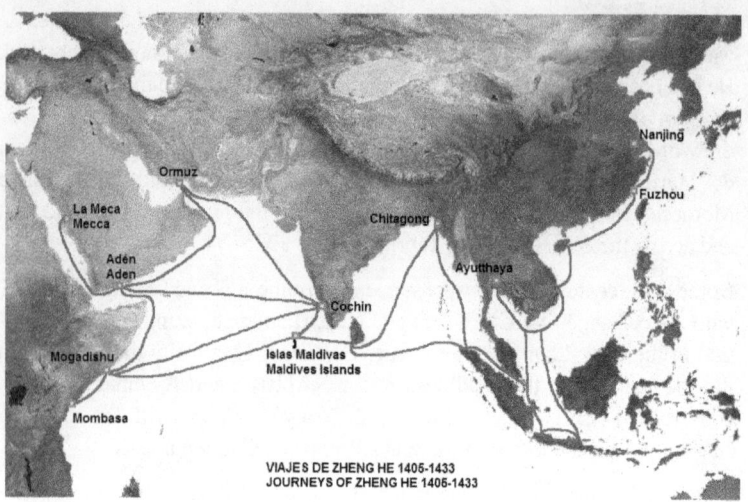

Figure 16: *Port cities on the maritime silk route featured on the voyages of Zheng He.*

New Silk Road

After an earthquake that hit Tashkent in Central Asia in 1966, the city had to rebuild itself. Although it took a huge toll on their markets, this commenced a revival of modern silk road cities.[79]

The Eurasian Land Bridge (a railway through China, Kazakhstan, Mongolia and Russia) is sometimes referred to as the "New Silk Road". The last link in one of these two railway routes was completed in 1990, when the railway systems of China and Kazakhstan connected at Alataw Pass (Alashan Kou). In 2008 the line was used to connect the cities of Ürümqi in China's Xinjiang Province to Almaty and Astana in Kazakhstan. In October 2008 the first Trans-Eurasia Logistics train reached Hamburg from Xiangtan. Starting in July 2011 the line has been used by a freight service that connects Chongqing, China with Duisburg, Germany, cutting travel time for cargo from about 36 days by container ship to just 13 days by freight train. In 2013, Hewlett-Packard began moving large freight trains of laptop computers and monitors along this rail route. In January 2017, the service sent its first train to London. The network additionally connects to Madrid and Milan.[80]

Figure 17: *A silk banner from Mawangdui, Changsha, Hunan province; it was draped over the coffin of Lady Dai (d. 168 BCE), wife of the Marquess Li Cang (利蒼) (d. 186 BCE), chancellor for the Kingdom of Changsha.*[78]

Belt and Road Initiative

In September 2013, during a visit to Kazakhstan, Chinese President Xi Jinping introduced a plan for a New Silk Road from China to Europe. The latest iterations of this plan, dubbed the "Belt and Road Initiative" (BRI), includes a land-based Silk Road Economic Belt and a 21st Century Maritime Silk Road, with primary points in Ürümqi, Dostyk, Astana, Gomel, the Belarussian city of Brest, and the Polish cities of Małaszewicze and Łódź—which would be hubs of logistics and transshipment to other countries of Europe.

On 15 February 2016, with a change in routing, the first train dispatched under the scheme arrived from eastern Zhejiang Province to Tehran. Though this section does not complete the Silk Road–style overland connection between China and Europe, plans are underway to extend the route past Tehran, through Istanbul, into Europe. The actual route went through Almaty, Bishkek, Samarkand, and Dushanbe.

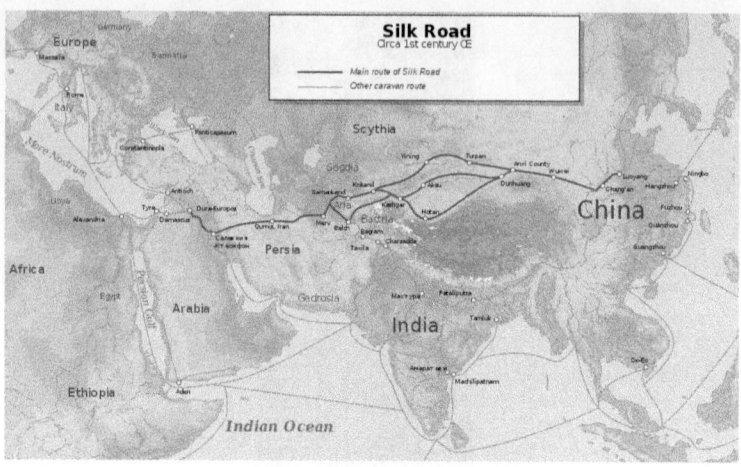

Figure 18: *The Silk Road in the 1st century*

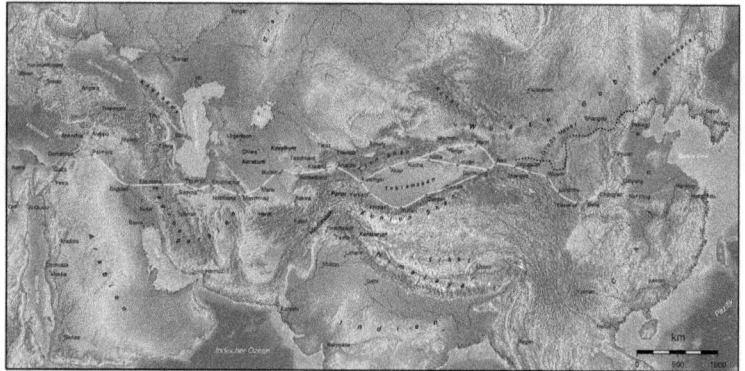

Figure 19: *The Silk Road*

Routes

The Silk Road consisted of several routes. As it extended westwards from the ancient commercial centres of China, the overland, intercontinental Silk Road divided into northern and southern routes bypassing the Taklamakan Desert and Lop Nur. Merchants along these routes where involved in "relay trade" in which goods changed "hands many times before reaching their final destinations."

Northern route

The northern route started at Chang'an (now called Xi'an), an ancient capital of China that was moved further east during the Later Han to Luoyang. The route was defined around the 1st century BCE when Han Wudi put an end to harassment by nomadic tribes.Wikipedia:Citation needed

The northern route travelled northwest through the Chinese province of Gansu from Shaanxi Province and split into three further routes, two of them following the mountain ranges to the north and south of the Taklamakan Desert to rejoin at Kashgar, and the other going north of the Tian Shan mountains through Turpan, Talgar, and Almaty (in what is now southeast Kazakhstan). The routes split again west of Kashgar, with a southern branch heading down the Alai Valley towards Termez (in modern Uzbekistan) and Balkh (Afghanistan), while the other travelled through Kokand in the Fergana Valley (in present-day eastern Uzbekistan) and then west across the Karakum Desert. Both routes joined the main southern route before reaching ancient Merv, Turkmenistan. Another branch of the northern route turned northwest past the Aral Sea and north of the Caspian Sea, then and on to the Black Sea.

A route for caravans, the northern Silk Road brought to China many goods such as "dates, saffron powder and pistachio nuts from Persia; frankincense, aloes and myrrh from Somalia; sandalwood from India; glass bottles from Egypt, and other expensive and desirable goods from other parts of the world."[81] In exchange, the caravans sent back bolts of silk brocade, lacquerware, and porcelain.

Southern route

The southern route or Karakoram route was mainly a single route from China through the Karakoram mountains, where it persists in modern times as the Karakoram Highway, a paved road that connects Pakistan and China.Wikipedia:Citation needed It then set off westwards, but with southward spurs so travelers could complete the journey by sea from various points. Crossing the high mountains, it passed through northern Pakistan, over the Hindu Kush mountains, and into Afghanistan, rejoining the northern route near Merv, Turkmenistan. From Merv, it followed a nearly straight line west through mountainous northern Iran, Mesopotamia, and the northern tip of the Syrian Desert to the Levant, where Mediterranean trading ships plied regular routes to Italy, while land routes went either north through Anatolia or south to North Africa. Another branch road travelled from Herat through Susa to Charax Spasinu at the head of the Persian Gulf and across to Petra and on to Alexandria and other eastern Mediterranean ports from where ships carried the cargoes to Rome.Wikipedia:Citation needed

Southwestern route

Woven silk textiles from Tomb No. 1 at Mawangdui, Changsha, Hunan province, China, Western Han dynasty period, dated 2nd century BCE

The southwestern route is believed to be the Ganges/Brahmaputra Delta, which has been the subject of international interest for over two millennia. Strabo, the 1st-century Roman writer, mentions the deltaic lands: "Regarding merchants who now sail from Egypt...as far as the Ganges, they are only private citizens..." His comments are interesting as Roman beads and other materials are being found at Wari-Bateshwar ruins, the ancient city with roots from much earlier, before the Bronze Age, presently being slowly excavated beside the Old Brahmaputra in Bangladesh. Ptolemy's map of the Ganges Delta, a remarkably accurate effort, showed that his informants knew all about the course of the Brahmaputra River, crossing through the Himalayas then bending westward to its source in Tibet. It is doubtless that this delta was a major international trading center, almost certainly from much earlier than the Common Era. Gemstones and other merchandise from Thailand and Java were traded in the delta and through it. Chinese archaeological writer Bin Yang and some earlier writers and archaeologists, such as Janice Stargardt, strongly suggest this route of international trade as Sichuan-Yunnan-Burma-Bangladesh route. According to Bin Yang, especially from the 12th century the route was used to ship bullion from Yunnan (gold and silver are among the minerals in which Yunnan is rich), through northern Burma, into modern Bangladesh, making use of the ancient route, known as the 'Ledo' route. The emerging evidence of the ancient cities of Bangladesh, in particular Wari-Bateshwar ruins, Mahasthangarh, Bhitagarh, Bikrampur, Egarasindhur, and Sonargaon, are believed to be the international trade centers in this route.[82]

Figure 20: *The Nestorian Stele, created in 781, describes the introduction of Nestorian Christianity to China*

Maritime route

Maritime Silk Road or Maritime Silk Route refer to the maritime section of historic Silk Road that connects China to Southeast Asia, Indonesian archipelago, Indian subcontinent, Arabian peninsula, all the way to Egypt and finally Europe.

The trade route encompassed numbers of bodies of waters; including South China Sea, Strait of Malacca, Indian Ocean, Gulf of Bengal, Arabian Sea, Persian Gulf and the Red Sea. The maritime route overlaps with historic Southeast Asian maritime trade, Spice trade, Indian Ocean trade and after 8th century – the Arabian naval trade network. The network also extend eastward to East China Sea and Yellow Sea to connect China with Korean Peninsula and Japanese archipelago.

Cultural exchanges

Richard Foltz, Xinru Liu, and others have described how trading activities along the Silk Road over many centuries facilitated the transmission not just of goods but also ideas and culture, notably in the area of religions. Zoroastrianism, Judaism, Buddhism, Christianity, Manichaeism, and Islam all spread across Eurasia through trade networks that were tied to specific religious communities and their institutions.[83] Notably, established Buddhist monasteries along the Silk Road offered a haven, as well as a new religion for foreigners.[84]

The spread of religions and cultural traditions along the Silk Roads, according to Jerry H. Bentley, also led to syncretism. One example was the encounter with the Chinese and Xiongnu nomads. These unlikely events of cross-cultural contact allowed both cultures to adapt to each other as an alternative. The Xiongnu adopted Chinese agricultural techniques, dress style, and lifestyle, while the Chinese adopted Xiongnu military techniques, some dress style, music, and dance.[85] Perhaps most surprising of the cultural exchanges between China and the Xiongnu, Chinese soldiers sometimes defected and converted to the Xiongnu way of life, and stayed in the steppes for fear of punishment.

Nomadic mobility played a key role in facilitating inter-regional contacts and cultural exchanges along the ancient Silk Roads.

Transmission of Christianity

The transmission of Christianity was primarily known as Nestorianism on the Silk Road. In 781, an inscribed stele shows Nestorian Christian missionaries arriving on the Silk Road. Christianity had spread both east and west, simultaneously bringing Syriac language and evolving the forms of worship.[86]

Transmission of Buddhism

The transmission of Buddhism to China via the Silk Road began in the 1st century CE, according to a semi-legendary account of an ambassador sent to the West by the Chinese Emperor Ming (58–75). During this period Buddhism began to spread throughout Southeast, East, and Central Asia.[90] Mahayana, Theravada, and Tibetan Buddhism are the three primary forms of Buddhism that spread across Asia via the Silk Road.

The Buddhist movement was the first large-scale missionary movement in the history of world religions. Chinese missionaries were able to assimilate Buddhism, to an extent, to native Chinese Daoists, which brought the two beliefs together.[91] Buddha's community of followers, the Sangha, consisted of male and female monks and laity. These people moved through India and beyond to spread the ideas of Buddha. As the number of members within the Sangha increased, it became costly so that only the larger cities were able to afford having the Buddha and his disciples visit.[92] It is believed that under the control of the Kushans, Buddhism was spread to China and other parts of Asia from the middle of the first century to the middle of the third century.[93] Extensive contacts started in the 2nd century, probably as a consequence of the expansion of the Kushan empire into the Chinese territory of the Tarim Basin,

Figure 21: *A blue-eyed Central Asian monk teaching an East-Asian monk, Bezeklik, Turfan, eastern Tarim Basin, China, 9th century; the monk on the right is possibly Tocharian,*[87] *although more likely Sogdian.*[88,89]

due to the missionary efforts of a great number of Buddhist monks to Chinese lands. The first missionaries and translators of Buddhists scriptures into Chinese were either Parthian, Kushan, Sogdian, or Kuchean.[94]

One result of the spread of Buddhism along the Silk Road was displacement and conflict. The Greek Seleucids were exiled to Iran and Central Asia because of a new Iranian dynasty called the Parthians at the beginning of the 2nd century BCE, and as a result the Parthians became the new middle men for trade in a period when the Romans were major customers for silk. Parthian scholars were involved in one of the first ever Buddhist text translations into the Chinese language. Its main trade centre on the Silk Road, the city of Merv, in due course and with the coming of age of Buddhism in China, became a major Buddhist centre by the middle of the 2nd century. Knowledge among people on the silk roads also increased when Emperor Ashoka of the Maurya dynasty (268–239 BCE) converted to Buddhism and raised the religion to official status in his northern Indian empire.

From the 4th century CE onward, Chinese pilgrims also started to travel on the Silk Road to India to get improved access to the original Buddhist scriptures, with Fa-hsien's pilgrimage to India (395–414), and later Xuanzang (629–644)

Figure 22: *Bilingual edict (Greek and Aramaic) by Indian Buddhist King Ashoka, 3rd century BCE; see Edicts of Ashoka, from Kandahar. This edict advocates the adoption of "godliness" using the Greek term Eusebeia for Dharma. Kabul Museum.*

and Hyecho, who traveled from Korea to India. The travels of the priest Xuanzang were fictionalized in the 16th century in a fantasy adventure novel called *Journey to the West*, which told of trials with demons and the aid given by various disciples on the journey.

There were many different schools of Buddhism travelling on the Silk Road. The Dharmaguptakas and the Sarvastivadins were two of the major Nikaya schools. These were both eventually displaced by the Mahayana, also known as "Great Vehicle". This movement of Buddhism first gained influence in the Khotan region. The Mahayana, which was more of a "pan-Buddhist movement" than a school of Buddhism, appears to have begun in northwestern India or Central Asia. It formed during the 1st century BCE and was small at first, and the origins of this "Greater Vehicle" are not fully clear. Some Mahayana scripts were found in northern Pakistan, but the main texts are still believed to have been composed in Central Asia along the Silk Road. These different schools and movements of Buddhism were a result of the diverse and complex influences and beliefs on the Silk Road. With the rise of Mahayana Buddhism, the initial direction of Buddhist development changed. This form of Buddhism

Figure 23: *A statue depicting Buddha giving a sermon, from Sarnath, 3,000 km (1,864 mi) southwest of Urumqi, Xinjiang, 8th century*

highlighted, as stated by Xinru Liu, "the elusiveness of physical reality, including material wealth." It also stressed getting rid of material desire to a certain point; this was often difficult for followers to understand.[95]

During the 5th and 6th centuries CE, merchants played a large role in the spread of religion, in particular Buddhism. Merchants found the moral and ethical teachings of Buddhism an appealing alternative to previous religions. As a result, merchants supported Buddhist monasteries along the Silk Road, and in return the Buddhists gave the merchants somewhere to stay as they traveled from city to city. As a result, merchants spread Buddhism to foreign encounters as they traveled.[96] Merchants also helped to establish diaspora within the communities they encountered, and over time their cultures became based on Buddhism. As a result, these communities became centers of literacy and culture with well-organized marketplaces, lodging, and storage.[97] The voluntary conversion of Chinese ruling elites helped the spread of Buddhism in East Asia and led Buddhism to become widespread in Chinese society.[98] The Silk Road transmission of Buddhism essentially ended around the 7th century with the rise of Islam in Central Asia.

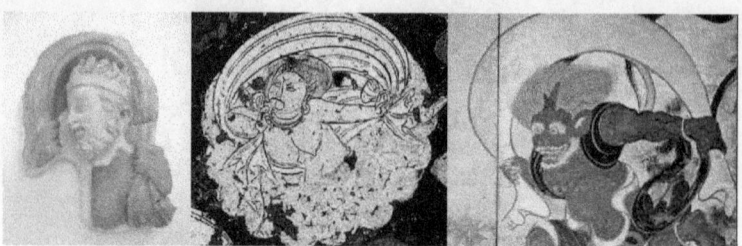

Figure 24: *Iconographical evolution of the Wind God. Left: Greek Wind God from Hadda, 2nd century. Middle: Wind God from Kizil, Tarim Basin, 7th century. Right: Japanese Wind God Fujin, 17th century.*

Transmission of art

Many artistic influences were transmitted via the Silk Road, particularly through Central Asia, where Hellenistic, Iranian, Indian and Chinese influences could intermix. Greco-Buddhist art represents one of the most vivid examples of this interaction. Silk was also a representation of art, serving as a religious symbol. Most importantly, silk was used as currency for trade along the silk road.[99]

These artistic influences can be seen in the development of Buddhism where, for instance, Buddha was first depicted as human in the Kushan period. Many scholars have attributed this to Greek influence. The mixture of Greek and Indian elements can be found in later Buddhist art in China and throughout countries on the Silk Road.

The production of art consisted of many different items that were traded along the Silk Roads from the East to the West. One common product, the lapis lazuli, was a blue stone with golden specks, which was used as paint after it was ground into powder.[100]

Commemoration

On 22 June 2014, the United Nations Educational, Scientific and Cultural Organization (UNESCO) named the Silk Road a World Heritage Site at the 2014 Conference on World Heritage. The United Nations World Tourism Organization has been working since 1993 to develop sustainable international tourism along the route with the stated goal of fostering peace and understanding.

Bishkek and Almaty each have a major east-west street named after the Silk Road (Kyrgyz: Жибек жолу, *Jibek Jolu* in Bishkek, and Kazakh: Жібек жолы, *Jibek Joly* in Almaty).

Foreign language terms

Language	Text	Transliteration (if applicable)
Chinese	絲綢之路 (traditional) 丝绸之路 (simplified)	Sīchóu zhī lù
Sanskrit / Hindi	कौशेय मार्ग	Kausheya Maraga
Persian	جاده ی ابریشم	Jâdeye Abrišam Shâhrâh-i Abrešim
Punjabi	ਕੌਸ਼ਿਆ ਮਾਰਗ	Kausheya Mārg
Urdu	شاہراہ ریشم	shah rah resham
Kannada	ರೇಷ್ಮೆ ದಾರಿ	Reshme dari
Kawi language	Sutra dalan	
Tamil	பட்டு வழி	Paṭṭu vaḻi
Uzbek	إيباك يولي	Ipak yo'li
Turkmen	Ýüpek ýoly	
Turkish	İpek yolu	
Azeri	İpək yolu	
Arabic	طريق الحرير	Tarīq al-Ḥarīr
Hebrew	המשי דרך	Derekh ha-Meshi
Greek	Δρόμος του μεταξιού	Drómos tou metaxioú'
Latin	Via Serica	
Armenian	Մետաքսի ճանապարհ	Metaksi chanaparh
Tagalog language	Daang Sutla, Daang Seda	
Somali language	وادادا وادادا	Waddada Waddada
Korean	비단길	Bidangil
Sinhala	සේද මාවත	Sedha mawatha

Gallery

Figure 25: *Caravanserai of Sa'd al-Saltaneh*

Figure 26: *Sultanhani caravanserai*

Figure 27: *Sultanhani caravanserai*

Figure 28: *Shaki Caravanserai, Azerbaijan*

Figure 29: *Orbelian's Caravanserai, Armenia*

Figure 30: *bridge in Ani, capital of medieval Armenia*

Figure 31: *Taldyk pass*

Figure 32: *Zeinodin Caravanserai*

Figure 33: *Sogdian man on a Bactrian camel, sancai ceramic glaze, Chinese Tang dynasty (618-907)*

Figure 34: *The ruins of a Han dynasty (206 BCE – 220 CE) Chinese watchtower made of rammed earth at Dunhuang, Gansu province*

Figure 35: *A late Zhou or early Han Chinese bronze mirror inlaid with glass, perhaps incorporated Greco-Roman artistic patterns*

Figure 36: *A Chinese Western Han dynasty (202 BCE – 9 CE) bronze rhinoceros with gold and silver inlay*

Figure 37: *Han dynasty Granary west of Dunhuang on the Silk Road.*

Figure 38: *Green Roman glass cup unearthed from an Eastern Han dynasty (25-220 CE) tomb, Guangxi, southern China*

References

Sources

<templatestyles src="Template:Refbegin/styles.css" />

- Baines, John and Málek, Jaromir (1984): *Atlas of Ancient Egypt*. Oxford, Time Life Books.
- Boulnois, Luce. 2004. *Silk Road: Monks, Warriors & Merchants on the Silk Road*. Translated by Helen Loveday with additional material by Bradley Mayhew and Angela Sheng. Airphoto International. <templatestyles src="Module:Citation/CS1/styles.css" />ISBN 962-217-720-4 hardback, <templatestyles src="Module:Citation/CS1/styles.css" />ISBN 962-217-721-2 softback.

- Ebrey, Patricia Buckley. (1999). *The Cambridge Illustrated History of China*. Cambridge: Cambridge University Press. <templatestyles src="Module:Citation/CS1/styles.css" />ISBN 0-521-66991-X.
- Foltz, Richard, *Religions of the Silk Road*, Palgrave Macmillan, 2nd edition, 2010, <templatestyles src="Module:Citation/CS1/styles.css" /> >ISBN 978-0-230-62125-1
- Harmatta, János, ed., 1994. *History of civilizations of Central Asia, Volume II. The development of sedentary and nomadic civilizations: 700 BC to 250*. Paris, UNESCO Publishing.
- Herodotus (5th century BCE): *Histories*. Translated with notes by George Rawlinson. 1996 edition. Ware, Hertfordshire, Wordsworth Editions Limited.
- Hopkirk, Peter: *Foreign Devils on the Silk Road: The Search for the Lost Cities and Treasures of Chinese Central Asia*. The University of Massachusetts Press, Amherst, 1980, 1984. <templatestyles src="Module:Citation/CS1/styles.css" />ISBN 0-87023-435-8
- Hill, John E. (2009) *Through the Jade Gate to Rome: A Study of the Silk Routes during the Later Han Dynasty, 1st to 2nd Centuries CE*. BookSurge, Charleston, South Carolina. <templatestyles src="Module:Citation/CS1/styles.css" />ISBN 978-1-4392-2134-1.
- Hulsewé, A. F. P. and Loewe, M. A. N. 1979. *China in Central Asia: The Early Stage 125 BC – 23: an annotated translation of chapters 61 and 96 of the History of the Former Han Dynasty*. E. J. Brill, Leiden.
- Huyghe, Edith and Huyghe, François-Bernard: "La route de la soie ou les empires du mirage", Petite bibliothèque Payot, 2006, <templatestyles src="Module:Citation/CS1/styles.css" />ISBN 2-228-90073-7
- Juliano, Annette, L. and Lerner, Judith A., et al. 2002. *Monks and Merchants: Silk Road Treasures from Northwest China: Gansu and Ningxia, 4th–7th Century*. Harry N. Abrams Inc., with The Asia Society. <templatestyles src="Module:Citation/CS1/styles.css" />ISBN 0-8109-3478-7; <templatestyles src="Module:Citation/CS1/styles.css" />ISBN 0-87848-089-7 softback.
- Klimkeit, Hans-Joach, im. 1988. *Die Seidenstrasse: Handelsweg and Kulturbruecke zwischen Morgen- and Abendland*. Koeln: DuMont Buchverlag.
- Klimkeit, Hans-Joachim. 1993. *Gnosis on the Silk Road: Gnostic Texts from Central Asia*. Trans. & presented by Hans-Joachim Klimkeit. HarperSanFrancisco. <templatestyles src="Module:Citation/CS1/styles.css" />ISBN 0-06-064586-5.
- Knight, E. F. 1893. *Where Three Empires Meet: A Narrative of Recent Travel in: Kashmir, Western Tibet, Gilgit, and the adjoining countries*. Longmans, Green, and Co., London. Reprint: Ch'eng Wen Publishing

Company, Taipei. 1971.
- Li, Rongxi (translator). 1995. *A Biography of the Tripiṭaka Master of the Great Ci'en Monastery of the Great Tang Dynasty*. Numata Center for Buddhist Translation and Research. Berkeley, California. <templatestyles src="Module:Citation/CS1/styles.css" />ISBN 1-886439-00-1
- Li, Rongxi (translator). 1995. *The Great Tang Dynasty Record of the Western Regions*. Numata Center for Buddhist Translation and Research. Berkeley, California. <templatestyles src="Module:Citation/CS1/styles.css" />ISBN 1-886439-02-8
- Litvinsky, B. A., ed., 1996. *History of civilizations of Central Asia, Volume III. The crossroads of civilizations: 250 to 750*. Paris, UNESCO Publishing.
- Liu, Xinru, 2001. "Migration and Settlement of the Yuezhi-Kushan: Interaction and Interdependence of Nomadic and Sedentary Societies." *Journal of World History*, Volume 12, No. 2, Fall 2001. University of Hawaii Press, pp. 261–92.[101].
- Liu, Li, 2004, *The Chinese Neolithic, Trajectories to Early States*, Cambridge UK, Cambridge University Press.
- Liu, Xinru (2010). *The Silk Road in World History*. Oxford University Press. <templatestyles src="Module:Citation/CS1/styles.css" />ISBN 978-0-19-516174-8; <templatestyles src="Module:Citation/CS1/styles.css" />ISBN 978-0-19-533810-2 (pbk).
- McDonald, Angus. 1995. *The Five Foot Road: In Search of a Vanished China*. HarperCollinsWest, San Francisco.
- Malkov, Artemy. 2007. The Silk Road: A mathematical model. *History & Mathematics*, ed. by Peter Turchin et al. Moscow: KomKniga. <templatestyles src="Module:Citation/CS1/styles.css" />ISBN 978-5-484-01002-8
- Mallory, J. P. and Mair, Victor H., 2000. *The Tarim Mummies: Ancient China and the Mystery of the Earliest Peoples from the West*. Thames & Hudson, London.
- Ming Pao. "Hong Kong proposes Silk Road on the Sea as World Heritage", 7 August 2005, p. A2.
- Osborne, Milton, 1975. *River Road to China: The Mekong River Expedition, 1866–73*. George Allen & Unwin Lt.
- Puri, B. N, 1987 *Buddhism in Central Asia*, Motilal Banarsidass Publishers Private Limited, Delhi. (2000 reprint).
- Ray, Himanshu Prabha, 2003. *The Archaeology of Seafaring in Ancient South Asia*. Cambridge University Press. <templatestyles src="Module:Citation/CS1/styles.css" />ISBN 0-521-80455-8 (hardback); <templatestyles src="Module:Citation/CS1/styles.css" />ISBN 0-521-01109-4 (paperback).

- Sarianidi, Viktor, 1985. *The Golden Hoard of Bactria: From the Tillyatepe Excavations in Northern Afghanistan.* Harry N. Abrams, New York.
- Schafer, Edward H. 1963. *The Golden Peaches of Samarkand: A study of T'ang Exotics.* University of California Press. Berkeley and Los Angeles. 1st paperback edition: 1985. <templatestyles src="Module:Citation/CS1/styles.css" />ISBN 0-520-05462-8.
- Stein, Aurel M. 1907. *Ancient Khotan: Detailed report of archaeological explorations in Chinese Turkestan*, 2 vols. Clarendon Press. Oxford.[102]
- Stein, Aurel M., 1912. *Ruins of Desert Cathay: Personal narrative of explorations in Central Asia and westernmost China*, 2 vols. Reprint: Delhi. Low Price Publications. 1990.
- Stein, Aurel M., 1921. *Serindia: Detailed report of explorations in Central Asia and westernmost China*, 5 vols. London & Oxford. Clarendon Press. Reprint: Delhi. Motilal Banarsidass. 1980.[102]
- Stein Aurel M., 1928. *Innermost Asia: Detailed report of explorations in Central Asia, Kan-su and Eastern Iran*, 5 vols. Clarendon Press. Reprint: New Delhi. Cosmo Publications. 1981.
- Stein Aurel M., 1932 *On Ancient Central Asian Tracks: Brief Narrative of Three Expeditions in Innermost Asia and Northwestern China.* Reprinted with Introduction by Jeannette Mirsky. Book Faith India, Delhi. 1999.
- Thorsten, Marie. 2006 "Silk Road Nostalgia and Imagined Global Community". Comparative American Studies 3, no. 3: 343–59.
- Waugh, Daniel. (2007). "Richthofen "Silk Roads": Toward the Archeology of a Concept." *The Silk Road.* Volume 5, Number 1, Summer 2007, pp. 1–10.[103]
- von Le Coq, Albert, 1928. Buried Treasures of Turkestan. Reprint with Introduction by Peter Hopkirk, Oxford University Press. 1985.
- Whitfield, Susan, 1999. *Life Along the Silk Road.* London: John Murray.
- Wimmel, Kenneth, 1996. *The Alluring Target: In Search of the Secrets of Central Asia.* Trackless Sands Press, Palo Alto, CA. <templatestyles src="Module:Citation/CS1/styles.css" />ISBN 1-879434-48-2
- Yan, Chen, 1986. "Earliest Silk Route: The Southwest Route." Chen Yan. *China Reconstructs*, Vol. XXXV, No. 10. October 1986, pp. 59–62.
- Yule (translator and editor), Sir Henry (1866). *Cathay and the way thither: being a collection of medieval notices of China. Issue 37 of Works issued by the Hakluyt Society*[104]. Printed for the Hakluyt society.<templatestyles src="Module:Citation/CS1/styles.css"></templatestyles>

Further reading

- Boulnois, Luce. Silk Road: Monks, Warriors and Merchants on the Silk Road[105]. Odyssey Publications, 2005. <templatestyles src="Module:Citation/CS1/styles.css" />ISBN 962-217-720-4
- Bulliet, Richard W. 1975. *The Camel and the Wheel*. Harvard University Press. <templatestyles src="Module:Citation/CS1/styles.css" />ISBN 0-674-09130-2.
- Christian, David (2000). "Silk Roads or Steppe Roads? The Silk Roads in World History". *Journal of World History*. University of Hawaii Press. 2.1 (Spring): 1.<templatestyles src="Module:Citation/CS1/styles.css"></templatestyles>
- de la Vaissière, E., Sogdian Traders. A History, Leiden, Brill, 2005, Hardback <templatestyles src="Module:Citation/CS1/styles.css" />ISBN 90-04-14252-5 Brill Publishers, French version <templatestyles src="Module:Citation/CS1/styles.css" />ISBN 2-85757-064-3 on[106]
- Elisseeff, Vadime. Editor. 1998. *The Silk Roads: Highways of Culture and Commerce*. UNESCO Publishing. Paris. Reprint: 2000. <templatestyles src="Module:Citation/CS1/styles.css" />ISBN 92-3-103652-1 softback; <templatestyles src="Module:Citation/CS1/styles.css" />ISBN 1-57181-221-0; <templatestyles src="Module:Citation/CS1/styles.css" />ISBN 1-57181-222-9 softback.
- Forbes, Andrew ; Henley, David (2011). *China's Ancient Tea Horse Road*. Chiang Mai: Cognoscenti Books. ASIN: B005DQV7Q2
- Frankopan, Peter. *The Silk Roads: A New History of the World* (2016). Very wide ranging scholarly survey, albeit without any maps.
- Hansen, Valerie. *The Silk Road: A New History* (Oxford University Press; 2012) 304 pages; Combines archaeology and history in a study of seven oases
- Hallikainen, Saana: *Connections from Europe to Asia and how the trading was affected by the cultural exchange* (2002)
- Hill, John E. (2004). *The Peoples of the West from the Weilüe* 魏略 *by Yu Huan* 魚豢 : *A Third Century Chinese Account Composed between 239 and 265*. Draft annotated English translation.[107]
- Hopkirk, Peter: *The Great Game: The Struggle for Empire in Central Asia*; Kodansha International, New York, 1990, 1992.
- Kuzmina, E. E. *The Prehistory of the Silk Road*. (2008) Edited by Victor H. Mair. University of Pennsylvania Press, Philadelphia. <templatestyles src="Module:Citation/CS1/styles.css" />ISBN 978-0-8122-4041-2
- Larsen, Jeanne. *Silk Road: A Novel of Eighth-Century China*. (1989; reprinted 2009)

- Levy, Scott C. (2012). "Early Modern Central Asia in World History". *History Compass*. **10** (11): 866–78. doi: 10.1111/hic3.12004[108].<templatestyles src="Module:Citation/CS1/styles.css"></templatestyles>
- Li et al. "Evidence that a West-East admixed population lived in the Tarim Basin as early as the early Bronze Age"[109]. *BMC Biology* 2010, 8:15.
- Liu, Xinru, and Shaffer, Lynda Norene. 2007. *Connections Across Eurasia: Transportation, Communication, and Cultural Exchange on the Silk Roads*. McGraw Hill, New York. <templatestyles src="Module:Citation/CS1/styles.css" />ISBN 978-0-07-284351-4.
- Miller, Roy Andrew (1959): *Accounts of Western Nations in the History of the Northern Chou Dynasty*. University of California Press.
- Omrani, Bijan; Tredinnick, Jeremy (2010). *Asia Overland: Tales of Travel on the Trans-Siberian and Silk Road*[110]. Hong Kong New York: Odyssey Distribution in the US by W.W. Norton & Co, Odyssey Publications. ISBN 962-217-811-1.<templatestyles src="Module:Citation/CS1/styles.css"></templatestyles>
- Polo, Marco, *Il Milione*.
- Thubron, C., *The Silk Road to China* (Hamlyn, 1989)
- Tuladhar, Kamal Ratna (2011). *Caravan to Lhasa: A Merchant of Kathmandu in Traditional Tibet*. Kathmandu: Lijala & Tisa. <templatestyles src="Module:Citation/CS1/styles.css" />ISBN 99946-58-91-3
- Watt, James C.Y.; Wardwell, Anne E. (1997). *When silk was gold: Central Asian and Chinese textiles*. New York: The Metropolitan Museum of Art. ISBN 0870998250.<templatestyles src="Module:Citation/CS1/styles.css"></templatestyles>
- Weber, Olivier, Eternal Afghanistan (photographs of Reza), (Unesco-Le Chêne, 2002)
- Yap, Joseph P. *Wars With the Xiongnu – A Translation From Zizhi Tongjian*. AuthorHouse (2009) <templatestyles src="Module:Citation/CS1/styles.css" />ISBN 978-1-4490-0604-4
- National Institute of Informatics – Digital Silk Road Project Digital Archive of Toyo Bunko Rare Books[102]
- Digital Silk Road > Toyo Bunko Archive > List of Books[111]

External links

 Wikimedia Commons has media related to *Silk Road*.

 Wikivoyage has a travel guide for *Silk Road*.

- Silk Road Atlas (University of Washington)[112]
- *The Silk Road*[113], a historical overview by Oliver Wild
- *The Silk Road Journal*[114], a freely available scholarly journal run by Daniel Waugh
- *The New Silk Road*[115] – a lecture by Paul Lacourbe at TEDxDanubia 2013
- Escobar, Pepe (February 2015). *Year of the Sheep, Century of the Dragon? New Silk Roads and the Chinese Vision of a Brave New (Trade) World*[116], an essay at Tom Dispatch

Cities along the Silk Road

Cities along the Silk Road

This articles lists **cities located along the Silk Road**. The Silk Road was a network of ancient trade routes which connected Europe with the Far East, spanning from the Mediterranean Sea to the Korean Peninsula and Japan.

Along the terrestrial/land Silk Roads

Major cities, broadly from the eastern Mediterranean to South Asia, and arranged roughly west to east in each area by modern-day country

The Silk Roads across the Middle East and Western Asia

Turkey

- Constantinople, ancient Byzantium, (now Istanbul), Roman Empire, Byzantine Empire & Ottoman Empire
- Bursa
- Beypazarı
- Mudurnu
- Taraklı
- Konya
- Adana
- Antioch
- Izmir
- Trabzon

Georgia

- Tbilisi (Tiflis)
- Batumi (Batoum)
- Poti

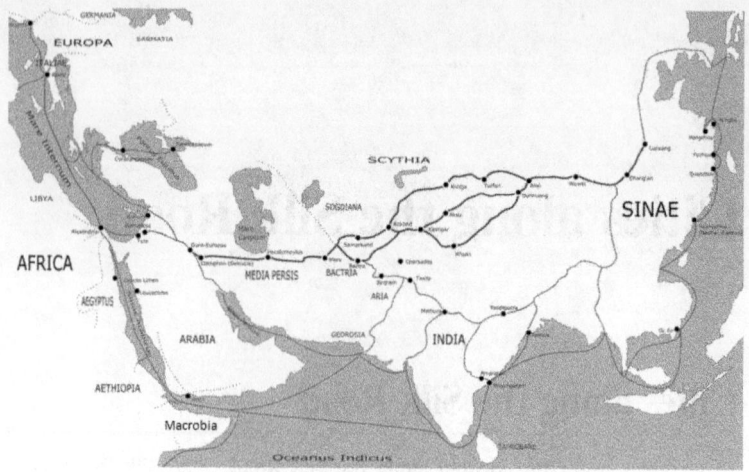

Figure 39: *The Silk Roads.*

Armenia

- Yerevan

Lebanon

- Tyre

Syria

- Aleppo
- Tartus
- Homs
- Damascus
- Palmyra
- Raqqa
- Dura Europos

Iraq

- Mosul
- Samarra
- Fallujah
- Baghdad
- Ctesiphon
- Baquba

Iran

- Tabriz

Figure 40: *Ruins of Muhammad II's palace in Old Urgench.*

- Zanjan
- Rasht
- Kermanshah
- Hamadan
- Rey (or Ray in modern-day Tehran)
- Hecatompylos (Damghan)
- Sabzevar
- Nishapur
- Mashhad
- Tus
- Bam
- Yazd
- Qazvin

Central Asia

Turkmenistan

- Nisa
- Merv
- Urgench
- Amul

Figure 41: *The Mausoleum of Khoja Ahmed Yasavi in the town of Hazrat-e Turkestan. Built by Timur in the 1390s.*

Uzbekistan

- Bukhara
- Shahrisabz
- Samarkand
- Tashkent
- Kokand (Fergana Valley)
- Andijon (Fergana Valley)

Tajikistan

- Khujand (Fergana Valley)
- Istaravshan

Kazakhstan

- Otrar
- Ispidjab (or Sairum)
- Taraz
- Hazrat-e Turkestan
- Almaty

Southern Routes and South Asia

Afghanistan

- Bactra (Balkh)
- Herat
- Alexandria Arachosia (Kandahar)
- Bamyan
- Kabul

Pakistan

- Quetta
- Pushkalavati/Peshawar
- Taxila
- Multan
- Debal/Banbhore/Barbarikon

India

- Leh
- Jaisalmer
- Mathura
- Varanasi (or Benares)
- Pataliputra

Nepal

- Kathmandu - see also Patan & Bhaktapur

Bangladesh

- Wari-Bateshwar
- Pundranagara
- Vikrampura
- Somapura
- Bhitargarh
- Sonargaon
- Chattagram/Chatgaon/Chittagong
- Comilla/Mainamati/Samatata
- Jahangir Nagar/Dhaka

Bhutan

- Jakar
- Paro

Figure 42: *The chain of cities along the northern route along the Taklamakan, probably based on Bento de Góis's itinerary, from Hiarcan (Yarkand) to Cialis (Karasahr or Korla) to Sucieu (Suzhou, Gansu)*

China: The northern route along the Taklamakan Desert

- Kashgar (or Kashi)
- Liqian
- Aksu
- Kucha
- Korla
- Loulan
- Karasahr (Yanqi)
- Turpan (Turfan)
  - *Jiaohe Ruins*
  - *Turpan Water Museum*
- Gaochang
  - *the Bezeklik Thousand Buddha Caves*
- Chang'an
- Kumul/Hami
- Ürümqi
- Yumen Pass (or Jade Gate or Pass of the Jade Gate) (city called Yumenguan or Hecang)
- Anxi

Cities along the Silk Road

Figure 43: *Map of eastern Xinjiang with prehistoric sites and the courses of the Folke Bergman, 1939*

China: The southern route along the Taklamakan Desert

- Kashgar (or Kashi)
- Yarkand
- Pishan
- Khotan
- Niya
- Mingfeng
- Endere
- Charchan
- Waxxari
- Ruoqiang Town (Charklik)
- Miran
- Yangguan, or Yangguan Pass
- Dunhuang
  - *the Mogao Caves*
- Anxi

Figure 44: *The ruins of a Han Dynasty (202 BC - 220 AD) Chinese watchtower made of rammed earth at Dunhuang, Gansu province, the eastern edge of the Silk Road*

China: From Anxi/Dunhuang to Chang'an (Xi'an)

- Dunhuang
- Jiayuguan
- Jiuquan
- Zhangye
- Shandan
- Liangzhou (Wuwei)
- Tianzhu, Gansu
- Lanzhou
- Tianshui
- Baoji
- Chang'an (modern-day Xi'an)

The eastern routes

Korea

- Pyongyang
- Gyeongju

Japan

- Nara

Along the maritime Silk Routes

- Debal, Pakistan
- Ningbo, China
- Fuzhou, China
- Quanzhou, China
- Guangzhou, China
- Ulsan, Korea
- Chittagong, Bangladesh
- Colombo, Sri Lanka
- Poompuhar, Tamil Nadu, India
- Madras, Tamil Nadu, India
- Korkai, Tamil Nadu, India
- Muziris, Kerala, India
- Goa, India
- Mumbai, India
- Cochin, India
- Masulipatnam, India
- Lothal, India
- Astrakhan, Russia
- Derbent, Russia
- Sudak, Russia
- Muscat, Oman
- Aden, Yemen
- Bosaso, Somalia
- Suez, Egypt
- Ayas, Turkey
- Venice, Italy
- Rome, Italy

In Southeast Asia

- Kedah (Early history of Kedah)
- Langkasuka
- Ligor
- Chi Tu
- Gangga Nagara
- Malacca
- Pan Pan
- Funan, Khmer
- Muziris, India
- Chenla, Khmer
- Vijaya of Champa

- Khmer / Kambuja
- Hanoi, Vietnam
- Hoi An, Vietnam
- Srivijaya, Indonesia
- Pasai, Indonesia
- Perlak, Indonesia

List of Ptolemy

 Wikimedia Commons has media related to *Cities along the Silk Road*.

This following list is attributed to Ptolemy. All city names are Ptolemy's, throughout all his works. Most of the names are included in *Geographia*.

Some of the cities provided by Ptolemy either

- do not longer exist today OR
- have moved to different locations

Nevertheless, Ptolemy has provided an important historical reference for researchers.

(*This list has been alphabetized.*)

- Africa
    - East Africa - Akhmim, Aromaton Emporion, Axum, Coloe, Dongola, Juba, Maji, Opone, Panopolis, Sarapion, Sennar.
    - North Africa - Caesarea, Carthage, Cyrene, Leptis Magna, Murzuk, Sijilmassa, Tamanrasset, Tingis.
- Arabia - Cane, Eudaemon Amrabia, Moscha, Mosyllon, Sana, Zafār (Saphar), Saue.
- Bangladesh - Sounagaora.
- China - Cattigara, Chengdu, Kaifeng, Kitai, Kunming, Yarkand.
- Europe - Aquileia, Athens, Augusta Treverorum (Trier), Gades (Cadiz), Ostia.
- India - Argaru, Astakapra, Bacare, Balita, Barake, Byzantion, Colchi, Erannoboas, Horaia, Kalliena, Mandagora, Melizeigara, Muziris, korkai, Poompuhar, Naura, Nelcynda, Paethana (Paithan), Palaepatmae, Palaesimundu, Poduca, Semylla, Sopatma, Suppara (Nalasopara), Tagara, Tymdis.
- Pakistan - Barbaricum, Peshawer, Taxilla
- Persia - Alexandria Areion, Kandahar, Persepolis.
- Persian Gulf - Apologos, Asabon, Charax, Gerrha (or Gerra), Ommana.

- Red Sea - Adulis, Aualites, Berenica, Malao, ancient Berbera, Muza, Myos Hormos, Ocalis, Ptolemais Theron.
- South East Asia - Kattigara (Oc Eo), Thaton, Trang.
- Unknown - Ecbatana (located in either modern Iran or Syria), Jiaohei.

Northern Silk Road

Northern Silk Road

The **Northern Silk Road** is a prehistoric trackway in northern China originating in the early capital of Xi'an and extending north of the Taklamakan Desert to reach the ancient kingdoms of Parthia, Bactria and eventually Persia and Rome.[117] It is the northern-most branch of several Silk Roads providing trade, military movements and cultural exchange between China and the west. The use of this route was expanded pursuant to actions by the Han Dynasty in the latter part of the first millennium BC to push back northern tribes and control the safe passage of Chinese troops and merchants.

Route

The route started at Chang'an (now called Xi'an), the capital of the Han Dynasty, which, in the Eastern Han, was moved further east to Luoyang. The route was defined about the 1st Century BCE as Han Wudi put an end to harassment by nomadic tribes.Wikipedia:Citation needed

The route travels northwest through the Chinese province of Gansu from Shaanxi Province, and splits into three further routes, two of them following the mountain ranges to the north and south of the Taklamakan Desert to rejoin at Kashgar; and the other going north of the Tian Shan mountains through Turpan, Talgar and Almaty (in what is now southeast Kazakhstan).

The routes split west of Kashgar with one branch heading down the Alay Valley towards Termez and Balkh, while the other traveled through Kokand in the Fergana Valley, and then west across the Karakum Desert towards Merv, joining the southern route briefly.

One of the branch routes turned northwest to the north of the Aral and Caspian seas and then on to the Black Sea.

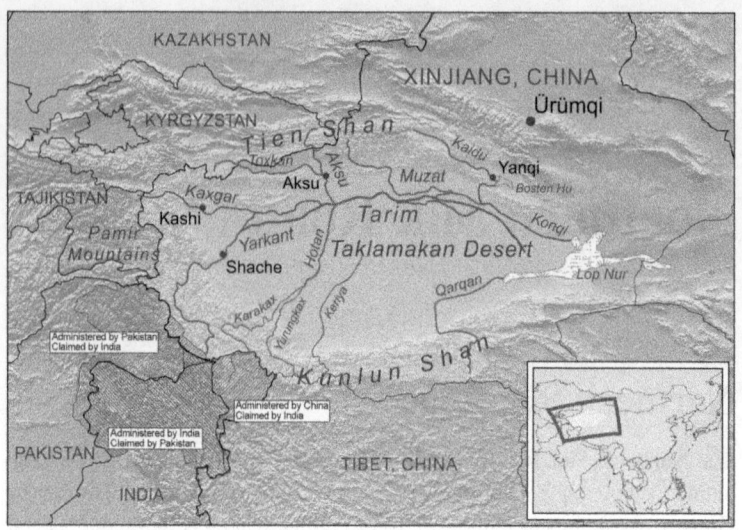

Figure 45: *Taklamakan Desert*

External links

- Pictures from the Northern Silk Road[118]

Tea Horse Road

Tea Horse Road

The **Tea Horse Road** or *chamadao* (simplified Chinese: 茶马道 ; traditional Chinese: 茶馬道), now generally referred to as the **Ancient Tea Horse Road** or *chamagudao* (simplified Chinese: 茶马古道 ; traditional Chinese: 茶馬古道) was a network of caravan paths winding through the mountains of Sichuan, Yunnan and Tibet in Southwest China.[119] This was also a tea trade route. It is also sometimes referred to as the **Southern Silk Road** or **Southwest Silk Road**, and it is part of a complex routes system connecting China and South Asia.

There are numerous surviving archaeological and monumental elements, including trails, bridges, way stations, market towns, palaces, staging posts, shrines and temples along the route. Besides the route's importance for commercial activity, more significantly it was crucial for cultural exchange between the Indian subcontinent, Tibet and Southwest China. Especially, it was vitally important for the interchange of Buddhism between China and South Asia.[120]

History

Sichuan and Yunnan are believed to be the first tea-producing regions in the world. The first record of tea cultivation in the world suggested that tea was cultivated on Sichuan's Mount Mengding (蒙顶山) between Chengdu and Ya'an earlier than 65 BC. Ya'an has been an important hub of tea trading till the 20th century. Besides tea, silk products from Chengdu, notably Shujin (蜀锦), was also traded through this road to South Asian from around 2000 years ago.

From around a thousand years ago, the Tea Horse Road was a trade link from Yunnan to Bengal via Burma; to Tibet; and to Central China via Sichuan Province. In addition to tea, the mule caravans carried salt. Both people and horses carried heavy loads, the tea porters sometimes carrying over 60–90 kg

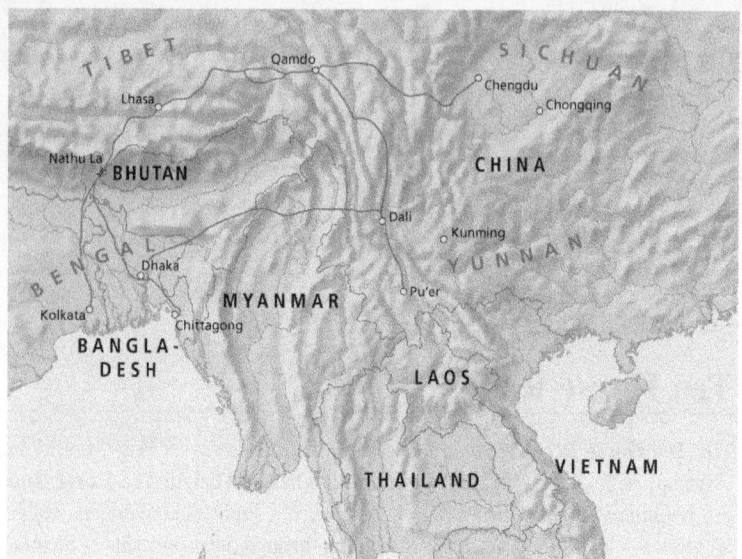

Figure 46: *Map of the Tea-Horse route*

Figure 47: *Men laden with tea, Sichuan Province, China, 1908, Ernest Henry Wilson*

(132-198 lb.), which was often more than their own body weight in tea. The porters carried metal-tipped staffs, both for balance while walking and to help support the load while they rested, so they didn't need to lay the bales down (as illustrated in the photo).

It is believed that it was through this trading network that tea (typically tea bricks) first spread across China and Asia from its origins in Pu'er county, near Simao Prefecture in Yunnan.[121,122]

The route earned the name Tea-Horse Road because of the common trade of Tibetan ponies for Chinese tea, a practice dating back at least to the Song dynasty, when the sturdy horses were important for China to fight warring nomads in the north.

Future

In the 21st century, the legacy of the Tea-Horse Road has been used to promote a railway that will connect Chengdu to Lhasa. This planned railroad, part of the PRC's 13th 5-Year Plan, is called the Sichuan-Tibet Railway (川藏铁路); it will connect cities across the route including Kangding. Authorities claim it will bring great benefit to the people's welfare.[123]

Gallery

Figure 48: *Feixiange Grottoes (689 AD), Buddhist art on the route from Chengdu to Ya'an.*

Figure 49: *The Royal Tea Garden, named by Emperor Xiaozong of Song (1186 AD) on Mount Mengding. Mount Mengding is the place where tea was first cultivated with written records (65 BC).*

Figure 50: *The surviving ancient route in Pujiang between Chengdu and Ya'an.*

Figure 51: *The historical site of Ganxipo Posthouse on the route in Tianquan, Sichuan.*

Figure 52: *The official tea warehouse of Tea Horse Bureau (Qing Dynasty) on the route in Tianquan, Sichuan.*

Figure 53: *The stone pagoda of Shita Temple (1169 AD) on the route from Chengdu to Ya'an.*

Figure 54: *Markham County in the very east of Tibet. In this region, near upper Mekong, there was the junction of the Sichuan and Yunnan branches of the route.*

Figure 55: *Mekong valley near Chamdo, where the river is crossed by the Tea-Horse-Route*

Figure 56: *Nathu La pass on the way from Lhasa to Calcutta*

Further reading

- Forbes, Andrew ; Henley, David (2011). *China's Ancient Tea Horse Road*. Chiang Mai: Cognoscenti Books. ASIN B005DQV7Q2[124]

- Forbes, Andrew ; Henley, David (2011). *Traders of the Golden Triangle*. Chiang Mai: Cognoscenti Books. ASIN B006GMID5[125]
- Freeman, Michael; Ahmed, Selena (2011). *Tea Horse Road: China's Ancient Trade Road to Tibet*. Bangkok: River Books Co, Ltd. ISBN 978-974-9863-93-0.<templatestyles src="Module:Citation/CS1/styles.css"></templatestyles>

External links

- Silk Road Foundation[126] - An authoritative article about the ancient tea route by Yang Fuquan, director of the Yunnan Academy of Social Sciences.
- Documentary: Insight on Asia - Asian Corridor in Heaven[127] - Made by KBS. TV Program.
- Tea Horse Road - National Geographic Magazine[128]
- "The Tea Horse Road"[129], Jeff Fuchs, *The Silk Road*, Vol.6, No.1 (Winter 2008).
- Interview: Jeff Fuchs[130], *Gokunming*, August 11, 2010.
- Bob Rogers and Claire Rogers[131], "Traveling Today's Tea Horse Road", Desert Leaf magazine, February 2011.

Maritime Silk Road

Maritime Silk Road

Maritime Silk Road or **Maritime Silk Route** refer to the maritime section of historic Silk Road that connects China to Southeast Asia, Indonesian archipelago, Indian subcontinent, Arabian peninsula, Somalia and all the way to Egypt and finally Europe, that flourished between 2nd-century BCE and 15th-century CE.

The trade route encompassed numbers of seas and ocean; including South China Sea, Strait of Malacca, Indian Ocean, Gulf of Bengal, Arabian Sea, Persian Gulf and the Red Sea. The maritime route overlaps with historic Southeast Asian maritime trade, Spice trade, Indian Ocean trade and after 8th century—the Arabian naval trade network. The network also extend eastward to East China Sea and Yellow Sea to connect China with Korean Peninsula and Japanese archipelago.

On May 2017, experts from various fields have held a meeting in London to discuss the proposal to nominate "Maritime Silk Route" as a new UNESCO World Heritage Site.

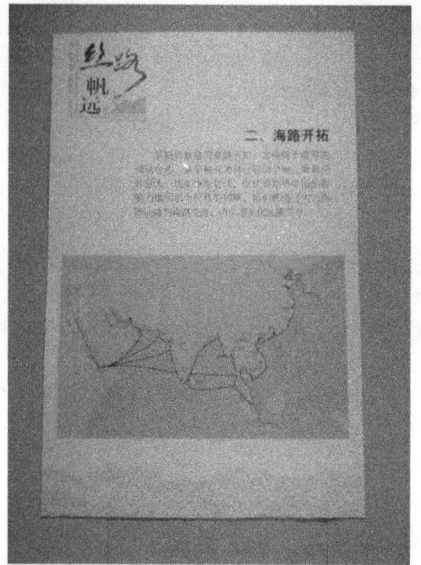

Figure 57: *The map of Maritime Silk Road*

Appendix

References

[1] http://whc.unesco.org/en/list/1442
[2] Xinru, Liu, *The Silk Road in World History* (New York: Oxford University Press, 2010), 11.
[3] Jerry Bentley, Old World Encounters: Cross-Cultural Contacts and Exchanges in Pre-Modern Times (New York: Oxford University Press, 1993), 32.
[4] Jerry Bentley, Old World Encounters: Cross-Cultural Contacts and Exchanges in Pre-Modern Times (New York: Oxford University Press, 1993), 33.
[5] Compare:
[6] Waugh (2007), p. 4.
[7] "Approaches Old and New to the Silk Roads" Eliseeff in: *The Silk Roads: Highways of Culture and Commerce*. Paris (1998) UNESCO, Reprint: Berghahn Books (2009), pp. 1–2. ; ; (pbk)
[8] "Approaches Old and New to the Silk Roads" Vadime Eliseeff in: *The Silk Roads: Highways of Culture and Commerce*. Paris (1998) UNESCO, Reprint: Berghahn Books (2000), pp. 1–2. ; ; (pbk)
[9] Waugh, Daniel. (2007). "Richthofen's "Silk Roads": Toward the Archaeology of a Concept." *The Silk Road*. Volume 5, Number 1, Summer 2007, p. 4.
[10] Warwick Ball (2016), *Rome in the East: Transformation of an Empire*, 2nd edition, London & New York: Routledge, , p. 156
[11] Warwick Ball (2016), *Rome in the East: Transformation of an Empire*, 2nd edition, London & New York: Routledge, , p. 155.
[12] Warwick Ball (2016), *Rome in the East: Transformation of an Empire*, 2nd edition, London & New York: Routledge, , pp. 154–56.
[13] Warwick Ball (2016), *Rome in the East: Transformation of an Empire*, 2nd edition, London & New York: Routledge, , pp. 155–56.
[14] (also available here)
[15] Christopoulos, Lucas (August 2012), "Hellenes and Romans in Ancient China (240 BC – 1398 AD)," in Victor H. Mair (ed), *Sino-Platonic Papers*, No. 230, Chinese Academy of Social Sciences, University of Pennsylvania Department of East Asian Languages and Civilizations, p. 31 footnote #56, .
[16] Hanks, Reuel R. (2010), *Global Security Watch: Central Asia*, Santa Barbara, Denver, Oxford: Praeger, p. 3.
[17] Mark J. Dresden (2003), "Sogdian Language and Literature", in Ehsan Yarshater, The Cambridge History of Iran, Vol III: The Seleucid, Parthian, and Sasanian Periods, Cambridge: Cambridge University Press, p. 1219, .
[18] Please refer to Royal Road.
[19] Christopoulos, Lucas (August 2012), "Hellenes and Romans in Ancient China (240 BC – 1398 AD)," in Victor H. Mair (ed), *Sino-Platonic Papers*, No. 230, Chinese Academy of Social Sciences, University of Pennsylvania Department of East Asian Languages and Civilizations, pp. 15–16, .
[20] Prevas, John. (2004). *Envy of the Gods: Alexander the Great's Ill-Fated Journey across Asia*, p. 121. De Capo Press, Cambridge, Mass.
[21] Jerry H. Bentley, *Old World Encounters: Cross-Cultural Contacts and Exchanges in Pre-Modern Times* (New York: Oxford University Press, 1993), 54.
[22] Di Cosmo,'Ancient China and its Enemies', 2002
[23] Ebrey (1999), 70.
[24] R. Ernest Dupuy and Trevor N. Dupuy, *The Harper Encyclopedia of Military History from 3500 B.C. to the Present*, Fourth Edition (New York: HarperCollins Publishers, 1993), 133, apparently relying on Homer H. Dubs, "A Roman City in Ancient China", in *Greece and Rome*, Second Series, Vol. 4, No. 2 (Oct., 1957), pp. 139–48
[25] Ban Chao http://www.britannica.com/EBchecked/topic/440601/Ban-Chao , Britannica Online Encyclopedia

[26] Frances Wood, *The Silk Road: Two Thousand Years in the Heart of Asia*, University of California Press, 2004, , p. 46

[27] Jerry H. Bentley, *Old World Encounters: Cross-Cultural Contacts and Exchanges in Pre-Modern Times* (New York: Oxford University Press, 1993), 32.

[28] An, Jiayao. (2002), "When Glass Was Treasured in China," in Annette L. Juliano and Judith A. Lerner (eds), *Silk Road Studies VII: Nomads, Traders, and Holy Men Along China's Silk Road*, 79–94, Turnhout: Brepols Publishers, , p. 83.

[29] de Crespigny, Rafe. (2007). *A Biographical Dictionary of Later Han to the Three Kingdoms (23–220 AD)*. Leiden: Koninklijke Brill, p. 600, .

[30] Yü, Ying-shih. (1986). "Han Foreign Relations," in Denis Twitchett and Michael Loewe (eds), *The Cambridge History of China: Volume I: the Ch'in and Han Empires, 221 B.C. –A.D. 220*, 377–462, Cambridge: Cambridge University Press, pp. 460–461, .

[31] An, Jiayao. (2002), "When Glass Was Treasured in China," in Annette L. Juliano and Judith A. Lerner (eds), *Silk Road Studies VII: Nomads, Traders, and Holy Men Along China's Silk Road*, 79–94, Turnhout: Brepols Publishers, , pp. 83–84.

[32] Harper, P.O. (2002), "Iranian Luxury Vessels in China From the Late First Millennium B.C.E. to the Second Half of the First Millennium C.E.," in Annette L. Juliano and Judith A. Lerner (eds), *Silk Road Studies VII: Nomads, Traders, and Holy Men Along China's Silk Road*, 95–113, Turnhout: Brepols Publishers, , pp. 106–07.

[33] Hansen, Valerie (2012), *The Silk Road: A New History*, Oxford: Oxford University Press, pp. 97–98, .

[34] Warwick Ball (2016), *Rome in the East: Transformation of an Empire*, 2nd edition, London & New York: Routledge, , p. 154.

[35] Helen Wang (2004) "Money on the Silk Road: The evidence from Eastern Central Asia to. c. AD 800," London: The British Museum Press, , p. 34.

[36] Gary K. Young (2001), *Rome's Eastern Trade: International Commerce and Imperial Policy, 31 BC – AD 305*, London & New York: Routledge, , p. 29.

[37] For further information on Oc Eo, see Milton Osborne (2006), *The Mekong: Turbulent Past, Uncertain Future*, Crows Nest: Allen & Unwin, revised edition, first published in 2000, , pp. 24–25.

[38] Ferdinand von Richthofen, *China*, Berlin, 1877, Vol.I, pp. 504–510; cited in Richard Hennig, *Terrae incognitae : eine Zusammenstellung und kritische Bewertung der wichtigsten vorcolumbischen Entdeckungsreisen an Hand der daruber vorliegenden Originalberichte, Band I, Altertum bis Ptolemäus*, Leiden, Brill, 1944, pp. 387, 410–11; cited in Zürcher (2002), pp. 30–31.

[39] Xinru Liu, *The Silk Road in World History* (New York: Oxford University Press, 2010), 21.

[40] " Strabo's Geography Book II Chapter 5 http://penelope.uchicago.edu/Thayer/E/Roman/Texts/Strabo/2E1*.html"

[41] Bharuch, Bharuch website, retrieved on 19 November 2013

[42] Barbarikon Karachi, Sindh, Pakistan website, retrieved on 19 November 2013.

[43] Xinru Liu, *The Silk Road in World History* (New York: Oxford University Press, 2010), 40.

[44] Pliny the Elder, *Natural Histories* 11.xxvi.76

[45] Xinru, Liu, *The Silk Road in World History* (New York: Oxford University Press, 2010), 21.

[46] Xinru Liu, The Silk Road in World History (New York: Oxford University Press, 2010), 75.

[47] Xinru, Liu, *The Silk Road in World History* (New York: Oxford University Press, 2010), p. 20

[48] Seneca the Younger (c. 3 BCE – 65 CE), Declamations Vol. I

[49] Sogdian Trade, *Encyclopedia Iranica*, (retrieved 15 June 2007) <>

[50] "Silk Road" http://www.livius.org/sh-si/silk_road/silk_road.html , LIVIUS Articles of Ancient History. 28 October 2010. Retrieved on 14 November 2010.

[51] Howard, Michael C. (2012), *Transnationalism in Ancient and Medieval Societies, the Role of Cross Border Trade and Travel*, McFarland & Company, p. 133.

[52] Mark J. Dresden (1981), "Introductory Note," in Guitty Azarpay, *Sogdian Painting: the Pictorial Epic in Oriental Art*, Berkeley, Los Angeles, London: University of California Press, p. 9, .

[53] Liu, Xinru, "The Silk Road: Overland Trade and Cultural Interactions in Eurasia", in Michael Adas (ed), *Agricultural and Pastoral Societies in Ancient and Classical History*, American Historical Association, Philadelphia: Temple University Press, 2001, p. 168.
[54] Luttwak, Edward N. (2009). *The Grand Strategy of the Byzantine Empire*. Cambridge and London: The Belknap Press of Harvard University Press. , pp. 168–69.
[55] Bretschneider, Emil (1888), *Medieval Researches from Eastern Asiatic Sources: Fragments Towards the Knowledge of the Geography and History of Central and Western Asia from the 13th to the 17th Century, Vol. 1*, Abingdon: Routledge, reprinted 2000, p. 144.
[56] Moule, A. C., *Christians in China before 1500*, 94 & 103; also Pelliot, Paul in *T'oung-pao* 15(1914), pp. 630–36.
[57] Peter Jackson (2005), The Mongols and the West, 1221–1410, Pearson Education, p. 169, .
[58] Kathleen Kuiper & editors of Encyclopædia Britannica (Aug 31, 2006). " Rabban bar Sauma: Mongol Envoy https://www.britannica.com/biography/Rabban-bar-Sauma ." *Encyclopædia Britannica* (online source). Accessed 16 September 2016.
[59] Morris Rossabi (2014). *From Yuan to Modern China and Mongolia: The Writings of Morris Rossabi*. Leiden & Boston: Brill, pp. 385–86, .
[60] Morris Rossabi (2014). *From Yuan to Modern China and Mongolia: The Writings of Morris Rossabi*. Leiden & Boston: Brill, pp. 386–421, .
[61] Luttwak, Edward N. (2009). *The Grand Strategy of the Byzantine Empire*. Cambridge and London: The Belknap Press of Harvard University Press. , p. 169.
[62] Luttwak, Edward N. (2009). *The Grand Strategy of the Byzantine Empire*. Cambridge and London: The Belknap Press of Harvard University Press. , pp. 169–70.
[63] Luttwak, Edward N. (2009). *The Grand Strategy of the Byzantine Empire*. Cambridge and London: The Belknap Press of Harvard University Press. , p. 170.
[64] Xinru Liu, The Silk Road in World History (New York: Oxford University Press, 2010), 68.
[65] Wink, André. Al-Hind: The Making of the Indo-Islamic World. Brill Academic Publishers, 2002.
[66] Dybo A.V., *"Chronology of Türkic languages and linguistic contacts of early Türks"*, Moskow, 2007, p. 786, https://web.archive.org/web/20050311224856/http://altaica.narod.ru/LIBRARY/xronol_tu.pdf
[67] Hanks, Reuel R. (2010), *Global Security Watch: Central Asia, Santa Barbara*, Denver, Oxford: Praeger, p. 4.
[68] Ebrey, Patricia Buckley; Walthall, Anne; Palais, James B. (2006), *East Asia: A Cultural, Social, and Political History*, Boston: Houghton Mifflin, , p. 100.
[69] Gascoigne, Bamber; Gascoigne, Christina (2003), *The Dynasties of China: A History*, New York: Carroll and Graf Publishers, an imprint of Avalon Publishing Group, , p. 97.
[70] Taenzer, Gertraud (2016), "Changing Relations between Administration, Clergy and Lay People in Eastern Central Asia: a Case Study According to the Dunhuang Manuscripts Referring to the Transition from Tibetan to Local Rule in Dunhuang, 8th–11th Centuries", in Carmen Meinert, *Transfer of Buddhism Across Central Asian Networks (7th to 13th Centuries)*, 19–56, Leiden, Boston: Brill, pp. 35–37, .
[71] Hanks, Reuel R. (2010), *Global Security Watch: Central Asia, Santa Barbara*, Denver, Oxford: Praeger, pp. 4–5.
[72] Sophie Ibbotson and Max Lovell-Hoare (2016), *Uzbekistan*, 2nd edition, Bradt Travel Guides Ltd, pp. 12–13, .
[73] Sophie Ibbotson and Max Lovell-Hoare (2016), *Uzbekistan*, 2nd edition, Bradt Travel Guides Ltd, pp. 14–15, .
[74] Xinru Liu, *The Silk Road in World History* (New York: Oxford University Press, 2010), 109.
[75] The Pax Mongolica http://www.silk-road.com/artl/paxmongolica.shtml , by Daniel C. Waugh, University of Washington, Seattle
[76] J. N. Hays (2005). " *Epidemics and pandemics: their impacts on human history https://books.google.com/books?id=GyE8Qt-kS1kC&pg=PA61* ". p.61.
[77] John Kelly, *The Great Mortality: An Intimate History of the Black Death, the Most Devastating Plague of All Time* (Harper: 2005).
[78] Hansen, Valerie (2000), *The Open Empire: A History of China to 1600*, New York & London: W.W. Norton & Company, , pp. 117–19

[79] Kathy Ceceri, *The Silk Road : Explore the World's Most Famous Trade Route* (White River Junction, VT: Nomad Press, 2011), 111.

[80] Silk Road route back in business as China train rolls into London https://www.theguardian.com/world/2017/jan/14/china-silk-road-trade-train-rolls-london , Tracy McVeigh, The Observer, 14 January 2017

[81] Ulric Killion, *A Modern Chinese Journey to the West: Economic Globalisation And Dualism*, (Nova Science Publishers: 2006), p.66

[82] Yang, Bin. (2008). *Between Winds and Clouds: The Making of Yunnan*. New York: Columbia University Press

[83] Richard Foltz, *Religions of the Silk Road*, New York: Palgrave Macmillan, 2nd edition, 2010,

[84] Xinru Liu, The Silk Road in World History (New York: Oxford University Press, 2010), 77.

[85] Jerry H. Bentley, *Old World Encounters: Cross-Cultural Contacts and Exchanges in Pre-Modern Times* (New York: Oxford University Press, 1993), 38.

[86] "Belief Systems Along the Silk Road," Asia Society website, , retrieved on November 14, 2016.

[87] von Le Coq, Albert. (1913). *Chotscho: Facsimile-Wiedergaben der Wichtigeren Funde der Ersten Königlich Preussischen Expedition nach Turfan in Ost-Turkistan* http://dsr.nii.ac.jp/toyobunko/LFc-42/V-1/page/0003.html.en . Berlin: Dietrich Reimer (Ernst Vohsen), im Auftrage der Gernalverwaltung der Königlichen Museen aus Mitteln des Baessler-Institutes, Tafel 19 http://dsr.nii.ac.jp/toyobunko/VIII-1-B-31/V-1/page-hr/0107.html.en . (Accessed 3 September 2016).

[88] Ethnic Sogdians have been identified as the Caucasian figures seen in the same cave temple (No. 9). See the following source: Gasparini, Mariachiara. " A Mathematic Expression of Art: Sino-Iranian and Uighur Textile Interactions and the Turfan Textile Collection in Berlin, http://heiup.uni-heidelberg.de/journals/index.php/transcultural/article/view/12313/8711#_edn32 " in Rudolf G. Wagner and Monica Juneja (eds), *Transcultural Studies*, Ruprecht-Karls Universität Heidelberg, No 1 (2014), pp. 134–63. See also . (Accessed 3 September 2016.)

[89] For information on the Sogdians, an Eastern Iranian people, and their inhabitation of Turfan as an ethnic minority community during the phases of Tang Chinese (7th–8th century) and Uyghur rule (9th–13th century), see Hansen, Valerie (2012), *The Silk Road: A New History*, Oxford University Press, p. 98, .

[90] Jerry H. Bentley, *Old World Encounters: Cross-Cultural Contacts and Exchanges in Pre-Modern Times* (New York: Oxford University Press, 1993), 69,73.

[91] Jerry Bentley, Old World Encounters: Cross-Cultural Contacts and Exchanges in Pre-Modern Times (New York: Oxford University Press, 1993), 16.

[92] Xinru Liu, "The Silk Road in World History" (New york: Oxford University Press, 2010), pp. 51.

[93] Xinru Liu, "The Silk Road in World History" (New York: Oxford University Press, 2010), pp. 42.

[94] Foltz, "Religions of the Silk Road", pp. 37–58

[95] Xinru Liu, "The Silk Road in World History" (New York: Oxford University Press, 2010), p. 21.

[96] Jerry H. Bentley, *Old World Encounters: Cross-Cultural Contacts and Exchanges in Pre-Modern Times* (New York: Oxford University Press, 1993), 43–44.

[97] Jerry H. Bentley, *Old World Encounters: Cross-Cultural Contacts and Exchanges in Pre-Modern Times* (New York: Oxford University Press, 1993), 48.

[98] Jerry H. Bentley, *Old World Encounters: Cross-Cultural Contacts and Exchanges in Pre-Modern Times* (New York: Oxford University Press, 1993), 50.

[99] Xinru, Liu,*The Silk Road in World History* (New York: Oxford University Press, 2010), 21.

[100] "The Silk Road and Beyond: Travel, Trade, and Transformation," Art Institute of Chicago website, , retrieved on 15 November 2016.

[101] http://muse.jhu.edu/journals/jwh/

[102] http://dsr.nii.ac.jp/toyobunko/

[103] http://www.silk-road.com/newsletter/vol5num1/srjournal_v5n1.pdf

[104] https://books.google.com/books?id=KzEMAAAAIAAJ

[105] https://books.google.com/books?id=issuAQAAIAAJ

[106] http://www.deboccard.com/

[107] http://depts.washington.edu/silkroad/texts/weilue/weilue.html
[108] //doi.org/10.1111%2Fhic3.12004
[109] https://web.archive.org/web/20110427172440/http://www.biomedcentral.com/content/pdf/1741-7007-8-15.pdf
[110] https://books.google.com/books?id=I7USQgAACAAJ
[111] http://dsr.nii.ac.jp/toyobunko/sitemap/index.html.en
[112] http://depts.washington.edu/silkroad/maps/maps.html
[113] http://arquivo.pt/wayback/20160315145417/http://www.ess.uci.edu/%7Eoliver/silk.html
[114] http://www.silk-road.com/toc/newsletter.html
[115] https://www.youtube.com/watch?v=97HlvtaWwik
[116] http://www.tomdispatch.com/post/175959/tomgram%3A_pepe_escobar%2C_inside_china%27s_%22new_normal%22/
[117] Gary K. Young, *Rome's Eastern Trade: International Commerce and Imperial Policy, 31 BC - AD 305*
[118] http://www.chrisrayn.com/collection/silk-road
[119] Forbes, Andrew, and Henley, David: *Traders of the Golden Triangle* (A study of the traditional Yunnanese mule caravan trade). Chiang Mai. Cognoscenti Books, 2011.
[120] Williams, Tim, Lin, Roland Chih-Hung and Gai, Jorayev. Final Technical Report on the results of the UNESCO/Korean Funds-in-Trust Project: Support for the Preparation for the World Heritage Serial Nomination of the Silk Roads in South Asia, 2013–2016.
[121] Jeff Fuchs. *The Ancient Tea Horse Road: Travels with the Last of the Himalayan Muleteers*, Viking Canada, 2008.
[122] Forbes, Andrew, and Henley, David, 'Pu'er Tea Traditions' in: *China's Ancient Tea Horse Road*. Chiang Mai, Cognoscenti Books, 2011.
[123] http://news.cntv.cn/2015/08/13/ARTI1439458357250340.shtml
[124] https://www.amazon.com/dp/B005DQV7Q2
[125] https://www.amazon.com/dp/B006GMID5
[126] http://www.silkroadfoundation.org/newsletter/2004vol2num1/tea.htm
[127] http://www.kbs.co.kr/1tv/sisa/insightasia/chama/
[128] http://ngm.nationalgeographic.com/2010/05/tea-horse-road/jenkins-text
[129] http://www.silk-road.com/newsletter/vol6num1/
[130] http://www.gokunming.com/en/blog/item/1732/interview_jeff_fuchs
[131] http://npaper-wehaa.com/desert-leaf#2011/02/01/?article=1144295:

Article Sources and Contributors

The sources listed for each article provide more detailed licensing information including the copyright status, the copyright owner, and the license conditions.

Silk Road *Source:* https://en.wikipedia.org/w/index.php?oldid=863367615 *License:* Creative Commons Attribution-Share Alike 3.0 *Contributors:* 23deshoa, 7&6=thirteen, A D Monroe III, Abdulrafeh857, Adam9007, ArglebargleIV, Artix Kreiger, BD2412, Babbage, BabelStone, Bbtknr, Begoon, Bongwarrior, BsBsBs, CASSIOPEIA, Callanecc, Cassa342, Chamboz, ChayaBH, Chewings72, ClueBot NG, Collectedtomes, Coolfish12, CurrentlyBoring, DRAGON BOOSTER, DVdm, DanielDanielShortdoLongdo, DatGoodDude342, Dawnseeker2000, Dearcabin21, Denisarona, DishkumTaka, Drmies, DuncanHill, Editsing123, Edward Mordake, Edward321, El cid, el campeador, Entranced98, Ermahgerd9, FATflash21, Favonian, Flooded with them hundreds, Flyer22 Reborn, Franrasyan, Frietjes, Ghostfacesecret, Gilliam, GoHyperMan, Gokudera ElPsyCongroo, GorillaWarfare, Gracomalfoy, Greyjoy, Gunkarta, Haldraper, Hayman30, I-Read-The-Dictonary, JC7V7DC5768, JMS Old Al, Joe Decker (alt), Johnbod, Jusdafix, KGirlTrucker81, KH-1, Kittywuver1000, Kuru, LakesideMiners, Laszlo Panaflex, LawrenceScafuri, Littlelago123, Loaka1, Look2See1, LouisAragon, MONGO, MaeseLeon, MagicSparklePlays, Majora, Mandruss, Marcocapelle, MarginalCost, Marianna251, Mark the train, Materialscientist, MaxEnt, Maximajorian Viridio, Miracle dream, Monopoly31121993, Nicat49, Ninjoust, Ogbrewer, Onel5969, Oshwah, PericlesofAthens, Peyre, Phenolla, Preslav, R'n'B, RHcosm, Rattans, RaviC, Red-eyed demon, Redgro, Reinstein17, Rjensen, SDC, Samantha Ireland, Samee, Samf4u, Scarabocchio, Seraphim System, Serols, Shellwood, Siddhartha 90, Simplexity22, SmartOne12345690, Spasage, Srich32977, SuNaW, Tahmina.tithi, Tar Lócesilion, Timmyshin, Titus III, Tomatopeel, Tomatopoteto, Trappist the monk, TwoTwoHello, VerifiedCactus, Visioncurve, Vsmith, WereSpielChequers, Wikivijimn, William Avery, Worldbruce, XPTO, YEAHBOIj, Yamaguchi先生, Ymblanter, Zachary Schr, ZeR0101MiNt, Виктор Јованоски, 207 anonymous edits 1

Cities along the Silk Road *Source:* https://en.wikipedia.org/w/index.php?oldid=861699419 *License:* Creative Commons Attribution-Share Alike 3.0 *Contributors:* Abbosali.abbosov, Alanl, Andrew Gray, Antimuonium, Appleby, Askhatekb, BD2412, Batternut, Bermicourt, Bonassra, BrownHairedGirl, CeeGee, Chapultepec, Chowbok, Chyah, Closedmouth, ClueBot NG, Cupla123, DabMachine, Deconstructhis, Delusion23, DemocraticLuntz, Dewritech, DivineAlpha, Donner60, Downwards, East of Borschov, Egmontaz, El cid, el campeador, Esmith6122, FayssalF, Folks at 137, FourteenDays, France3470, Fratrep, Fredrick2920, Ghepeu, Ghirlandajo, Gilliam, Googoo0202, Gorthian, Grafen, Guy1890, HaeB, HeCTiiC HuNTeR, Himraz, Historiographer, Homora, Hrh80, I dream of horses, ILovePlankton, ImmortalWombat, ImpuMozhi, Instantnood, J04n, Jamesmcmahon0, Jared Preston, Jluu~enwiki, Jschnur, Kelvin Case, Kmzayeem, Koumz, L joo, Latebird, Leathp, Lotje, Mark Arsten, Mark the train, Materialscientist, Mattise, Mean as custard, Merchant of Asia, Merv1221, Mjpieters, Mr. Guye, Mr. Smart LION, MusikAnimal, N1RK4UDSK714, Niceguyedc, Nick Number, Ninetyone, Niteowlneils, Nlu, NottNott, Npeters22, Onel5969, Oshwah, Parabolooidal, Paxse, Per Honor et Gloria, Philip Trueman, PhnomPencil, Pinethicket, Polyxeros, RA0808, Rajiv7280, Rjanag, Rodw, Roylee, RuiPang, Sahmeditor, Sangjinhwa, SchreiberBike, ShelfSkewed, Siddiqui, Skeeter451, Skinsmoke, Sololackey, Soranoch, Soroush Mesry, Sunray, The Banner, The best Checker, Tillerh11, Tomdo08, Utcursch, Vanjagenije, Vegeta428, Vmenkov, Walter Holden-Belmont, Wiae, Wiki13, Winner 42, Woohookitty, Wtmitchell, Xaosflux, Ymblanter, Ynsars, ZZyXx, ZackTheJack, 198 anonymous edits 47

Northern Silk Road *Source:* https://en.wikipedia.org/w/index.php?oldid=768972943 *License:* Creative Commons Attribution-Share Alike 3.0 *Contributors:* Ahuskay, Bdiscoe, Beetstra, Cattus, Fleebo, Greg Grahame, Hunnjazal, J 1982, JaGa, Katineee, MadameArsenic, Mary*wu, Parabolooidal, Sevilledade, Steven J. Anderson, Stikkyy, TruckCard, Pjóóólfr, 6 anonymous edits 59

Tea Horse Road *Source:* https://en.wikipedia.org/w/index.php?oldid=845841652 *License:* Creative Commons Attribution-Share Alike 3.0 *Contributors:* 40fifw0, AndrewHowse, Asfroeas, Blaylockjam10, Brandmeister, Cameralumina, CanadianLinuxUser, Chris the speller, Dale662, Davidcannon, Dcirovic, Delirium, Derek R Bullamore, Dthomsen8, Earthlyreason, Endgame1, Faulah, Gabbe, Gaia1CB3, Ghirlandajo, GreenC, Havelock the Dane, J 1982, Jalo, Jaxartes, John Prattley, Johnsoniensis, Ju66l3r, Klemen Kocjancic, LogAntiLog, Lotje, Marcocapelle, Materialscientist, McGeddon, Mlondon, Mz7, Philafrenzy, R'n'B, Redgeographics, Robertirogers, Ronz, Rédacteur Tibet, Scriberius, Secretteadrinker, Sesquepedalia, Sevilledade, ShelfSkewed, SimonP, Sjschen, Slimey3000, Takeaway, Tazikipedia, Tijuana Brass, Ulamm, Underbar dk, Vmenkov, WOSlinker, Xiefeilaga, Yerius J, Zanhe, Zujine, ٢٠١٢م ابراهيم, 日本一世, 琴竹, 40 anonymous edits 61

Maritime Silk Road *Source:* https://en.wikipedia.org/w/index.php?oldid=861844212 *License:* Creative Commons Attribution-Share Alike 3.0 *Contributors:* Cold Season, Gunkarta, Jonpatterns, LiberatorG, RevelationDirect, 6 anonymous edits 69

Image Sources, Licenses and Contributors

The sources listed for each image provide more detailed licensing information including the copyright status, the copyright owner, and the license conditions.

Image *Source:* https://en.wikipedia.org/w/index.php?title=File:Padlock-silver.svg *Contributors:* AzaToth, BotMultichill, BotMultichillT, Gurch, Jarekt, Kallerna, Multichill, Perhelion, Rd232, Riana, Sarang, Siebrand, Steinsplitter, 4 anonymous edits 1

Image *Source:* https://en.wikipedia.org/w/index.php?title=File:Silk_route.jpg *License:* Public Domain *Contributors:* User:HighInBC 1

Figure 1 *Source:* https://en.wikipedia.org/w/index.php?title=File:Woven_silk,_Western_Han_Dynasty.jpg *License:* Public Domain *Contributors:* Chinese artist 2

Figure 2 *Source:* https://en.wikipedia.org/w/index.php?title=File:ChineseJadePlaques.JPG *License:* Creative Commons Attribution-ShareAlike 3.0 Unported *Contributors:* User:World Imaging 4

Figure 3 *Source:* https://en.wikipedia.org/w/index.php?title=File:Map_achaemenid_empire_en.png *License:* Creative Commons Attribution-Sharealike 2.5 *Contributors:* User:Fabienkhan 5

Figure 4 *Source:* https://en.wikipedia.org/w/index.php?title=File:UrumqiWarrior.jpg *License:* Public Domain *Contributors:* Ismoon (talk) 23:05, 20 December 2012 (UTC) 6

Figure 5 *Source:* https://en.wikipedia.org/w/index.php?title=File:HanHorse.jpg *License:* Public Domain *Contributors:* BotAdventures, BrightRaven, Ismoon, Kersti Nebelsiek, Kilom691, PericlesofAthens, Sailko, Shauni, Thib Phil, Underwaterbuffalo, Zolo 8

Figure 6 *Source:* https://en.wikipedia.org/w/index.php?title=File:Bronze_coin_of_Contantius_II_337_361_found_in_Karghalik.jpg *License:* Public Domain *Contributors:* Uploadalt 8

Figure 7 *Source:* https://en.wikipedia.org/w/index.php?title=File:Seidenstrasse_GMT_Ausschnitt_Zentralasien.jpg *License:* GNU Free Documentation License *Contributors:* Chyah, Firespeaker, Flawed reality, Jean11, Look2See1, MGA73bot2, Maksim, McPot, NordNordWest, Sarang, Sprachpfleger, Stewi101015, Warburg, Yuriy75, Zykasaa, 2 anonymous edits 11

Figure 8 *Source:* https://en.wikipedia.org/w/index.php?title=File:Cernuschi_Museum_20060812_150.jpg *License:* Creative Commons Attribution-Sharealike 3.0,2.5,2.0,1.0 *Contributors:* Guillaume Jacquet 12

Figure 9 *Source:* https://en.wikipedia.org/w/index.php?title=File:Solidus_Constans_II_(obverse).jpg *License:* GNU Free Documentation License *Contributors:* Jeff G., Marcus Cyron, SJuergen, Tuvalkin 14

Figure 10 *Source:* https://en.wikipedia.org/w/index.php?title=File:ForeignerWithWineskin-Earthenware-TangDynasty-ROM-May8-08.png *License:* Creative Commons Attribution-ShareAlike 3.0 Unported *Contributors:* User:Captmondo 15

Figure 11 *Source:* https://en.wikipedia.org/w/index.php?title=File:Caravane_sur_la_Route_de_la_soie_-_Atlas_catalan.jpg *License:* Public Domain *Contributors:* Cresques Abraham 16

Figure 12 *Source:* https://en.wikipedia.org/w/index.php?title=File:Radhanites2.png *License:* Creative Commons Attribution 2.5 *Contributors:* Briangotts 17

Figure 13 *Source:* https://en.wikipedia.org/w/index.php?title=File:Baghdad_150_to_300_AH.gif *Contributors:* - 18

Figure 14 *Source:* https://en.wikipedia.org/w/index.php?title=File:Lions,_soie_polychrome_sogdienne,_Asie_centrale.jpg *License:* Public Domain *Contributors:* Aschroet, OgreBot 2, PericlesofAthens, Yann 19

Figure 15 *Source:* https://en.wikipedia.org/w/index.php?title=File:Travels_of_Marco_Polo.svg *License:* Creative Commons Attribution-Sharealike 3.0 *Contributors:* Asie.svg: historicair 20:31, 20 November 2006 (UTC) derivative work: Classical geographer (talk) 20

Figure 16 *Source:* https://en.wikipedia.org/w/index.php?title=File:Zheng_He.png *License:* Creative Commons Attribution-Sharealike 3.0 *Contributors:* User:Continentalis 22

Figure 17 *Source:* https://en.wikipedia.org/w/index.php?title=File:Mawangdui_silk_banner_from_tomb_no1.jpg *License:* Public Domain *Contributors:* Cold Season, Huangdan2060, LlywelynII, Yann 23

Figure 18 *Source:* https://en.wikipedia.org/w/index.php?title=File:Silk_Road_in_the_I_century_AD_-_en.svg *Contributors:* Babbage 24

Figure 19 *Source:* https://en.wikipedia.org/w/index.php?title=File:SeidenstrasseGMT.JPG *License:* Creative Commons Attribution-Sharealike 3.0 *Contributors:* Kelvin Case 24

Image *Source:* https://en.wikipedia.org/w/index.php?title=File:Silk_from_Mawangdui_2.jpg *License:* Creative Commons Attribution-Sharealike 2.0 *Contributors:* drs2biz 26

Image *Source:* https://en.wikipedia.org/w/index.php?title=File:Silk_from_Mawangdui.jpg *License:* Public Domain *Contributors:* drs2biz 26

Figure 20 *Source:* https://en.wikipedia.org/w/index.php?title=File:Nestorian-Stele-Budge-plate-X.jpg *License:* Public Domain *Contributors:* Nestorian monk Jingjing. Rubbing/drawing made by Henri Havret, or a local collaborator of his 27

Figure 21 *Source:* https://en.wikipedia.org/w/index.php?title=File:Central_Asian_Buddhist_Monks.jpeg *Contributors:* of the paintings - Unknown. Of the book, Albert von Le Coq. 29

Figure 22 *Source:* https://en.wikipedia.org/w/index.php?title=File:AsokaKandahar.jpg *License:* Public Domain *Contributors:* Abhishekjoshi, Archidamus∼commonswiki, BotAdventures, BotMultichill, Fertejol, Frenezulo, Gryffindor, Iustinus, JMCC1, Jastrow, Jdx, Le Behnam, Mahmudmasri, Man vyi, Mikhail Ryazanov, Mmcannis∼commonswiki, Officer, Ranveig, Roland zh, Sreejithk2000 AWB, Storkk, Tahar Jelun, The Evil IP address, Wieralee, Wiki-uk, World Imaging, Zaccarias, ZxxZxxZ, पाटलिपुत्र, 17 anonymous edits 30

Figure 23 *Source:* https://en.wikipedia.org/w/index.php?title=File:A_statue_depicting_Buddha_giving_sermon,_from_Sarnath,_now_at_Museum_of_Asian_Art,_Dahem_Berlin.jpg *License:* Creative Commons Attribution 2.0 *Contributors:* Jean-Pierre Dalbéra 31

Figure 24 *Source:* https://en.wikipedia.org/w/index.php?title=File:WindGods.JPG *License:* Public Domain *Contributors:* Aotake, Kilom691, MGA73bot2, Man vyi, Shizhao, Takeaway, Un1c0s bot∼commonswiki, 1 anonymous edits 32

Figure 25 *Source:* https://en.wikipedia.org/w/index.php?title=File:Caravanserai_of_Sa'd_al-Saltaneh_1.jpg *Contributors:* User:Parastoo.Atrsaei 34

Figure 26 *Source:* https://en.wikipedia.org/w/index.php?title=File:Sultanhani_Caravanserai,_Turkey1.jpg *License:* Creative Commons Attribution-Sharealike 2.0 *Contributors:* Dennis Jarvis from Halifax, Canada 34

Figure 27 *Source:* https://en.wikipedia.org/w/index.php?title=File:Caravasar_de_Sultanhani._Han.jpg *License:* Creative Commons Attribution 3.0 *Contributors:* José Luis Filpo Cabana 35

Figure 28 *Source:* https://en.wikipedia.org/w/index.php?title=File:Caravanserai-Sheki.jpg *License:* Creative Commons Attribution-Sharealike 2.0 *Contributors:* AudreyH 35

Figure 29 *Source:* https://en.wikipedia.org/w/index.php?title=File:Selim_Pass_Caravanserai_(5127896201).jpg *License:* Creative Commons Attribution-Sharealike 2.0 *Contributors:* Shaun Dunphy from Lindfield, United Kingdom 35

Figure 30 *Source:* https://en.wikipedia.org/w/index.php?title=File:The_remains_of_a_bridge2.jpg *License:* Creative Commons Attribution-Sharealike 2.0 *Contributors:* Steven Isaacson from Somerville, MA, USA 36

Figure 31 *Source:* https://en.wikipedia.org/w/index.php?title=File:Taldyk_pass_(3600_m).jpg *License:* Creative Commons Attribution 2.0 *Contributors:* Gustavo Jeronimo from Aranjuez, Spain 36

Figure 32 *Source:* https://en.wikipedia.org/w/index.php?title=File:Zeinodin_Caravanserai.jpg *License:* Creative Commons Attribution 2.0 *Contributors:* David Stanley 37

Figure 33 *Source:* https://en.wikipedia.org/w/index.php?title=File:Westerner_on_a_camel.jpg *License:* Public domain *Contributors:* Airunp, BrokenSphere, Conscious, Daderot, Enatrix, Howcheng, Ismoon, Johnbod, Lilyu, Michael Gäbler, Olivier, PericlesofAthens, Smooth O, World Imaging, Wst, Zolo, 1 anonymous edits 37

Figure 34 *Source:* https://en.wikipedia.org/w/index.php?title=File:Summer_Vacation_2007,_263,_Watchtower_In_The_Morning_Light,_Dunhuang,_Gansu_Province.jpg *License:* Creative Commons Attribution 2.0 *Contributors:* The Real Bear 38

Figure 35 *Source:* https://en.wikipedia.org/w/index.php?title=File:WhiteHanBronzeMirror.JPG *License:* GNU Free Documentation License *Contributors:* BabelStone, BotAdventures, Daderot, Jastrow, Johnbod, MGA73bot2, PericlesofAthens, Sailko, World Imaging, 1 anonymous edits 38

Figure 36 *Source:* https://en.wikipedia.org/w/index.php?title=File:Xihan_rhino,_gold_&_silver_inlays.JPG *License:* Creative Commons Attribution-Share Alike *Contributors:* Gary Lee Todd 39

Figure 37 *Source:* https://en.wikipedia.org/w/index.php?title=File:Han_Dynasty_Granary_west_of_Dunhuang.jpg *License:* Creative Commons Attribution-Sharealike 3.0 *Contributors:* User:John Hill 40

Figure 38 *Source:* https://en.wikipedia.org/w/index.php?title=File:Green_glass_Roman_cup_unearthed_at_Eastern_Han_tomb,_Guixian,_China.jpg *License:* Public Domain *Contributors:* User:John Hill 40

Image *Source:* https://en.wikipedia.org/w/index.php?title=File:Commons-logo.svg *License:* logo *Contributors:* Anomie, Callanecc, CambridgeBayWeather, Jo-Jo Eumerus, RHaworth 46

Image *Source:* https://en.wikipedia.org/w/index.php?title=File:Wikivoyage-Logo-v3-icon.svg *License:* Creative Commons Attribution-Sharealike 3.0 *Contributors:* User:AleXXw 46

Figure 39 *Source:* https://en.wikipedia.org/w/index.php?title=File:Transasia_trade_routes_1stC_CE_gr2.png   *License:* Creative Commons Attribution-ShareAlike 3.0 Unported *Contributors:* Anna Frodesiak, Annam Imperatoria, BotMultichill, CommonsDelinker, Davepape, Dudu90, G.dallorto, It Is Me Here, Kaidor, Karlfk, Kritikklinge, LlywelynII, Longbow4u, Mayhaymate, Nagy, Newone, Roland zh, Runehelmet, Shizhao, Warburg, Zykasaa, Шухрат Сатьпиев, 13 anonymous edits 48
Figure 40 *Source:* https://en.wikipedia.org/w/index.php?title=File:Urgench.jpg *License:* GNU Free Documentation License *Contributors:* Lohen11, MBxd1, MGA73bot2, N. Wadid, OgreBot 2, Olivier 49
Figure 41 *Source:* https://en.wikipedia.org/w/index.php?title=File:View_of_the_Mosque_of_Hazrat_in_the_town_of_Turkestan.JPG *License:* Public Domain *Contributors:* Butko, Celeron, Ctac, Fred J, Kandar, Man vyi, N. Wadid, Olivier, Rd232, Vizu, Wst, Yuriy75 50
Figure 42 *Source:* https://en.wikipedia.org/w/index.php?title=File:CEM-36-NW-corner.jpg *License:* Public Domain *Contributors:* Giacomo Cantelli (1643-1695), Giovanni Giacomo de Rossi (17th century) 52
Figure 43 *Source:* https://en.wikipedia.org/w/index.php?title=File:Map_of_eastern_Xinjiang_1939_with_prehistoric_sites_and_the_courses_of_the_Silk_Roads.jpg *License:* Creative Commons Attribution 2.5 *Contributors:* Folke Bergman 53
Figure 44 *Source:* https://en.wikipedia.org/w/index.php?title=File:Summer_Vacation_2007,_263,_Watchtower_In_The_Morning_Light,_Dunhuang,_Gansu_Province.jpg *License:* Creative Commons Attribution 2.0 *Contributors:* The Real Bear 54
Figure 45 *Source:* https://en.wikipedia.org/w/index.php?title=File:Tarimrivermap.png *License:* Creative Commons Attribution-Sharealike 3.0 *Contributors:* Kmusser 60
Figure 46 *Source:* https://en.wikipedia.org/w/index.php?title=File:Map_of_the_Tea-Horse_road.png *License:* GNU Free Documentation License *Contributors:* Redgeographics 62
Figure 47 *Source:* https://en.wikipedia.org/w/index.php?title=File:Men_Laden_With_Tea,_Sichuan_Sheng,_China_1908_Ernest_H._Wilson_RESTORED.jpg *License:* Creative Commons Attribution 2.0 *Contributors:* ralph repo 62
Figure 48 *Source:* https://en.wikipedia.org/w/index.php?title=File:□□□□□□.JPG *Contributors:* User:Nekitarc 63
Figure 49 *Source:* https://en.wikipedia.org/w/index.php?title=File:□□.JPG *Contributors:* User:Nekitarc 64
Figure 50 *Source:* https://en.wikipedia.org/w/index.php?title=File:□□□□□□.jpg *Contributors:* User:Nekitarc 64
Figure 51 *Source:* https://en.wikipedia.org/w/index.php?title=File:□□□□□□□□□□.jpg *Contributors:* User:Nekitarc 65
Figure 52 *Source:* https://en.wikipedia.org/w/index.php?title=File:□□□.jpg *Contributors:* User:Nekitarc 65
Figure 53 *Source:* https://en.wikipedia.org/w/index.php?title=File:□□□□□.jpg *Contributors:* User:Nekitarc 65
Figure 54 *Source:* https://en.wikipedia.org/w/index.php?title=File:Markam_County_Tibet.jpg *License:* Creative Commons Attribution 2.0 *Contributors:* Reurinkjan 66
Figure 55 *Source:* https://en.wikipedia.org/w/index.php?title=File:Chamdo_Mekong.png *License:* Creative Commons Attribution-Sharealike 3.0 *Contributors:* Jaryiahr Khan 66
Figure 56 *Source:* https://en.wikipedia.org/w/index.php?title=File:Nathu_La.jpg *License:* Creative Commons Attribution 2.0 *Contributors:* Giridhar Appaji Nag Y 67
Figure 57 *Source:* https://en.wikipedia.org/w/index.php?title=File:□□□_□□□□□□.JPG *License:* Creative Commons Attribution-Sharealike 3.0 *Contributors:* User:Davidzdh 70

License

Creative Commons Attribution-Share Alike 3.0
//creativecommons.org/licenses/by-sa/3.0/

Index

Abbasid, 21
Abbasid Caliphate, 19
Abbasid dynasty, 18
Achaemenid Empire, 5
Achaemenid Persian Empire, 5
Adana, 47
Aden, 55
Adulis, 57
Aegean Sea, 5
Afghanistan, 2, 6, 51
Africa, 56
Akhmim, 56
Aksum, 16
Aksu, Xinjiang, 52
Alans, 9
Alashankou Railway Station, 22
Alay Valley, 59
Albert von Le Coq, 74
Aleppo, 48
Alexander the Great, 6
Alexandria, 25
Alexandria Arachosia, 51
Alexandria Areion, 56
Alexandria Eschate, 6
Almaty, 22, 25, 32, 50, 59
Al-Mukalla, 56
Amazon Standard Identification Number, 67, 68
Anatolia, 19, 25
Ancient Egypt, 4
Ancient Greek philosophy, 6
Ancient history, 2
Ancient Rome, 10, 11
Andijon, 50
Andrew of Longjumeau, 21
Andronikos II Palaiologos, 14
Ani, 36
Animal style, 4
An Lushan Rebellion, 19
Antioch, 47
Antoninus Pius, 10
Anxi (archaeological site), 53
Anxi (Arsacid territories), 52
Anxi County, 7

Apologos, 56
Aquileia, 56
Arabia, 2, 16, 56
Arabian peninsula, 27, 69
Arabian Sea, 27, 69
Arabic, 33
Arabs, 2
Aral Sea, 25, 59
Aramaic, 30
Argaru, 56
Arghun, 14
Arimaspians, 3
Armenia, 36, 48
Armenian language, 33
Armenians, 2, 16
Aromaton Emporion, 56
Asabon, 56
Ashina tribe, 17
Assyria, 5
Astakapra, 56
Astana, 22
Astrakhan, 18, 55
Aswan, 5
Athens, 56
Aualites, 57
Augusta Treverorum, 56
Augustus, 11
Aurelian, 10
Axum, 56
Ayas (city), 55
Ayyubid, 21
Azerbaijan, 35
Azerbaijanis, 2, 33

Bacare, 56
Bactria, 2, 6, 7, 59
Bactrian camel, 38
Badakhshan, 3
Baghdad, 18, 48
Bagram, 13
Bagratid Armenia, 36
Balita, 56
Balkh, 25, 51, 59
Bam, Iran, 49

Bamyan, Afghanistan, 51
Banbhore, 51
Ban Chao, 10
Bangladesh, 26, 51, 55, 56
Baoji, 54
Baquba, 48
Barake, 56
Barbarikon, 51, 56
Battle of Talas, 19
Batumi, 47
Beijing, 18
Belt and Road Initiative, 23
Benedykt Polak, 21
Bengal, 61
Bento de Góis, 52
Berbera, 57
Berenice Troglodytica, 57
Beypazarı, Ankara, 47
Bezeklik, 29
Bezeklik Thousand Buddha Caves, 52
Bhaktapur, 51
Bharuch, 72
Bhitagarh, 26
Bhitargarh, 51
Bijan Omrani, 45
Bikrampur, 26, 51
Bishkek, 23, 32
Black Death, 21
Black Sea, 4, 25, 59
BMC Biology, 45
Boris Anatolevich Litvinsky, 42
Bosaso, 55
Bota bag, 15
Brahmaputra, 26
Brest, Belarus, 23
Brill Publishers, 44
British Museum, 4
Bronze Age, 26
Bronze sculpture, 4
Buddhism, 18, 61
Buddhism in Central Asia, 19, 29
Bukhara, 9, 19, 50
Burma, 26, 61
Bursa, 47
Byzantine emperor, 14
Byzantine Empire, 10, 13, 16, 47
Byzantine silk, 13
Byzantion, 56
Byzantium, 47

Cadiz, 56
Cádiz, 56
Caesar Augustus, 9
Caesarea, 56
Caesar (title), 13
Calcutta, 67

Cambodia, 55, 56
Cambridge University Press, 71
Caravanserai, 35
Caravanserai of Sad al-Saltaneh, 34
Caravan to Lhasa, 45
Carpathian Mountains, 5
Carthage, 56
Caspian Sea, 10, 25, 59
Cattigara, 56
Centaur, 6
Central Asia, 2, 4, 6, 32
Central China, 61
Chamdo, 67
Champa, 55
Changan, 10, 25, 52, 54, 59
Changsha, 2, 23, 26
Charax Spasinu, 25, 56
Chengdu, 56, 61, 63
Chenla, 55
China, 2, 3, 8, 27, 52–54, 56, 59, 61, 63, 69
China Proper, 7
Chinese art, 32
Chinese language, 14, 33
Chinese nobility, 14
Chinese people, 2
Chinese Turkestan, 6
Chittagong, 51, 55
Chi Tu, 55
Chongqing, 22
Cities along the Silk Road, 18, **47**
Classical Greece, 6
Cochin, 55
Colchi, 56
Coloe, 56
Colombo, 55
Columbia University Press, 74
Comilla, 51
Commons:Category:Cities along the Silk Road, 56
Commons:Silk Road, 46
Conquest of the Western Turks, 16
Constans II, 13, 14
Constantinople, 13, 47
Constantius II, 8
Crimea, 19
Crossbow, 9
Crusades, 21
Ctesiphon, 18, 48
Cyrene, Libya, 56

Damascus, 18, 48
Damghan, 49
Daniel Waugh (historian), 46
Daqin, 10, 13
Daxia, 7
Dayuan, 7

Debal, 51, 55
De:Keshengzhuang, 4
Derbent, 55
Dhaka, 51
Dharma, 30
Diaspora, 31
Dionysus, 10
Dominate, 10
Dongola, 56
Dostyk, 23
Duisburg, 22
Dunhuang, 19, 40, 53, 54
Dura Europos, 48
Dushanbe, 23

Early history of Kedah, 55
East Africa, 2, 56
East Asia, 2
East China Sea, 27, 69
Eastern Han dynasty, 8, 25, 40, 59
Eastern Iranian people, 74
Eastern world, 1
Ecbatana, 57
Edicts of Ashoka, 30
Edward Gibbon, 3
Edward I of England, 14
Egypt, 5, 27, 69
Emil Bretschneider, 14
Emperor Gaozong of Tang, 15
Emperor Huan of Han, 10
Emperor Ming of Han, 28
Emperor Shenzong of Song, 13
Emperor Taizong of Tang, 13, 15
Emperor Taizongs campaign against Tuyuhun, 15
Emperor Taizongs campaign against Xueyantuo, 15
Emperor Wu of Han, 15
Emperor Wu of Han China, 7
Emperor Xiaozong of Song, 64
Empress Wu, 15
Endere, 53
En:Digital object identifier, 45
Entrepôt, 20
Erannoboas, 56
Ernest Henry Wilson, 62
Erzurum, 19
Esarhaddon, 5
Ethiopia, 16
Eudaemon Amrabia, 56
Eudoxus of Cyzicus, 11
Euphrates, 16
Eurasian Land Bridge, 22
Europe, 2, 27, 56, 69
Europeans in Medieval China, 3
Eusebeia, 30

Euthydemus I, 6

Fa-hsien, 29
Fallujah, 48
Far East, 21, 47
Ferdinand von Richthofen, 3, 11
Fergana Valley, 6, 7, 25, 50, 59
Ferghana, 7
File:BezeklikSogdianMerchants.jpg, 74
First Roman embassy, 10
Florus, 9
Folke Bergman, 53
Former Soviet republics, 3
Four Garrisons of Anxi, 15
Franco-Mongol alliance, 14, 21
Frankincense, 25
Friedrich Hirth, 14
Fūjin, 32
Fuzhou, 55

Ganges, 26
Ganges Delta, 26
Gangga Nagara, 55
Gansu, 10, 19, 25, 59
Gan Ying, 10
Gaochang, 52
Gao Xianzhi, 15
Gastraphetes, 9
Gemstones, 26
Genghis Khan, 14, 19
Geography (Ptolemy), 11, 56
Georgia (country), 47
Georgian people, 2
Georgics, 12
Germany, 4
Gerrha, 56
Giao Chỉ, 10
Gilgit, 15
Giovanni da Pian del Carpine, 21
Giovanni de Marignolli, 21
Glass, 39
Goa, 55
Göktürk, 15
Göktürks, 17
Gomel, 23
Granary, 40
Greater Iran, 10
Greater Persia, 2
Great Hungarian Plain, 5
Great Wall of China, 2
Greco-Bactrian, 7
Greco-Bactrian Kingdom, 6, 9
Greco-Buddhism, 6
Greco-Buddhist art, 32
Greek language, 30, 33
Greeks, 2, 6

Guangxi, 40
Guangzhou, 10, 17, 55
Guiyi Circuit, 19
Gulf of Bengal, 27, 69
Gunpowder, 21
Gyeongju, 11, 12, 54

Hadda, Afghanistan, 32
Hamadan, 49
Hamburg, 22
Han dynasty, 2, 7, 40, 54, 59
Han–Xiongnu War, 7
Hanoi, 10, 11, 56
Han Wudi, 25, 59
Harvard University Press, 44
Hazrat-e Turkestan, 50
Hebrew language, 33
Hecatompylos, 49
Helen Wang, 72
Hellenistic, 32
Hellenistic period, 6
Henry Yule, 10
Herat, 25, 51
Herodotus, 5, 41
Hewlett-Packard, 22
Hexi Corridor, 7, 19
Himalayas, 26
Hindi, 33
Hindu Kush, 25
History, 63
History Compass, 45
History of Ming, 14
History of silk, 23
History of Song, 13
History of the Han dynasty, 2
History of Yuan, 13
Hoi An, 56
Holy Land, 21
Homs, 48
Hongwu Emperor, 14
Hopkirk, Peter, 41
Horaia, 56
Horn of Africa, 2, 16
Hotan, 53
Hou Junji, 15
Hunan, 2, 23, 26
Hyecho, 30

Ibn Battuta, 21
Ilkhanate, 21
Il Khanate, 16
India, 2, 10, 51, 55, 56
Indian art, 32
Indian Ocean, 17, 27, 69
Indian Ocean trade, 27, 69
Indian people, 2

Indian subcontinent, 27, 61, 69
Indo-Greek Kingdom, 6
Indonesia, 27, 69
Indo-Roman trade relations, 3, 10
Inner Asia, 3
Inner Mongolia, 4
International Standard Book Number, 40–45, 68
Ionians, 7
Iran, 25, 48, 57
Iranian peoples, 2
Iraq, 16, 48
Iron Curtain, 3
Islam, 18
Islamic world, 19
Istämi, 13
Istanbul, 23, 47
Istaravshan, 50
Italy, 25

İzmir, 5, 47

Jade, 3, 4
Jahangir Nagar, 51
Jaisalmer, 51
Jakar, 51
János Harmatta, 41
Japan, 2, 47, 54
Japanese archipelago, 27, 69
Java, 26
Jeff Fuchs, 68, 75
Jerry H. Bentley, 28, 71, 72, 74
Jews, 2
Jiaohei, 57
Jiaohe Ruins, 52
Jiaozhi, 10
Jiaozhou (region), 10
Jiayuguan City, 54
Jingyuan County, Gansu, 10
Jiuquan, 54
John of Montecorvino, 14, 21
John V Palaiologos, 14
Journal of World History, 42, 44
Journey to the West, 30
Juba, Southern Sudan, 56
Judaism, 27
Justinian, 13
Justin II, 13

Kabul, 30, 51
Kaifeng, 56
Kalliena, 56
Kambuja, 56
Kanchipuram, 16
Kandahar, 30, 51, 56
Kangju, 7

Kannada, 33
Kannur, 56
Kansu, 5
Kara-Khanid Khanate, 19
Karakoram, 25
Karakoram Highway, 25
Karakorum (palace), 18, 20
Karakum Desert, 25, 59
Karasahr, 7, 52
Kargilik Town, 8
Karun, 5
Kashgar, 6, 25, 52, 53, 59
Kathmandu, 51
Kattigara, 11, 57
Kawi language, 33
Kazakh language, 32
Kazakhstan, 3, 22, 25, 50, 59
Kazan, 19
Kermanshah, 49
Khanbaliq, 13
Khosrow I, 13
Khotan, 3, 30
Khujand, 50
Kingdom of Funan, 10, 55
Kingdom of Qocho, 74
Kings of the Han dynasty, 23
Kizil Caves, 32
Kokand, 25, 50, 59
Konya, 47
Konye-Urgench, 49
Korea, 2, 54
Korean Broadcasting System, 68
Korean language, 33
Korean Peninsula, 27, 47, 69
Korkai, 55, 56
Korla, 52
Kublai Khan, 13
Kucha, 7, 52
Kuchean, 29
Kumul (city), 52
Kunming, 56
Kushan, 28
Kushan Empire, 13
Kyrgyz language, 32
Kyrgyzstan, 19

Lady Dai, 23
Langkasuka, 55
Lanzhou, 54
Lapis lazuli, 3, 32
Larsen, Jeanne, 44
Late Antiquity, 10
Later Han History, 7
Latin, 33
Lebanon, 48
Leh, 51

Leptis Magna, 56
Levant, 25
Lhasa, 63, 67
Light cavalry, 10
Ligor, 55
Li Jing (Tang dynasty), 15
Lingua franca, 5
Liqian (village), 52
List of World Heritage Sites in Asia, 1

Łódź, 23

London, 22
Lop Nur, 24
Lothal, 55
Louis Malleret, 11
Loulan (town), 52
Luoyang, 10, 25, 59

Madras, 55
Madrid, 22
Maes Titianus, 11
Magyars, 16
Mahasthangarh, 26, 51
Mainamati, 51
Maji, Ethiopia, 56
Malacca, 55
Malao (ancient), 57
Małaszewicze, 23
Malay people, 2
Mamluk Sultanate (Cairo), 21
Mandagora, 56
Manichaeism, 18, 19
Marc Aurel Stein, 43
Marco Polo, 3, 20
Marcus Aurelius, 10
Maritime history, 69
Maritime Silk Road, **69**
Markam County, 66
Mark Antony, 9
Mashhad, 49
Masulipatnam, 55
Mathura, 51
Mausoleum of Khoja Ahmed Yasavi, 50
Mawangdui, 2, 23, 26
Medal, 10
Mediterranean, 4
Mediterranean Sea, 25, 47
Mekong, 66, 67
Melizeigara, 56
Merchants, 31
Merv, 25, 29, 49, 59
Mesopotamia, 7, 9, 16, 25
Metropolitan regions of China, 4
Michael VII Doukas, 13
Middle East, 4, 47

Milan, 22
Military, 59
Minfeng Town, 53
Ming dynasty, 14
Miran (China), 53
Mocha, Yemen, 56, 57
Mogao Caves, 53
Monarchy, 59
Mongol conquest of Khwarezmia, 19
Mongol Empire, 3, 18, 19
Mongol invasions, 20
Morocco, 21
Mosul, 48
Mosyllon, 56
Motif (textile arts), 19
Mounted infantry, 10
Mount Mengding, 64
Mudurnu, 47
Muhammad II of Khwarezm, 49
Multan, 51
Mumbai, 55
Murzuk, 56
Muscat, Oman, 55
Muslim, 21
Muslim conquest of Transoxiana, 19
Muziris, 55, 56
Myos Hormos, 11, 57
Myrrh, 25

Nabataean, 10
Nalasopara, 56
Nanjing, 10
Nara, Nara, 54
Nathu La, 67
Natural Histories, 12
Nelcynda, 56
Nepal, 51
Nephrite, 3
Nestorian, 14
Nestorian Christianity, 13, 19
Nestorian Church, 18
Nestorian Stele, 27
New Book of Tang, 13
Niccolò de Conti, 21
Ningbo, 55
Nisa, Turkmenistan, 49
Nishapur, 49
Niya (Tarim Basin), 53
North Africa, 25, 56
Northern Silk Road, **59**
Northern Wei dynasty, 12
North Pakistan, 6

Ocalis (city), 57
Oc Eo, 57, 72

Óc Eo, 10

Odoric of Pordenone, 21
Odyssey Publications, 45
Old Book of Tang, 13
Old Urgench, 49
Olivier Weber, 45
Ommana, 56
Opone, 56
Orbelians Caravanserai, 36
Ostia Antica, 56
Otrar, 50
Ottoman Empire, 21, 47
Oxford University Press, 71
Oxus, 16

Paethana, 56
Paithan, 56
Pakistan, 6, 51, 56
Palaepatmae, 56
Palaesimundu, 56
Palmyra, 48
Pamir Mountains, 3
Pamirs, 10
Panopolis, 56
Pan Pan (kingdom), 55
Paro, Bhutan, 51
Parthia, 9, 12, 29, 59
Parthian Empire, 7, 29
Pasai, 56
Pataliputra, 51
Patan, Nepal, 51
Pax Sinica, 16
Pepe Escobar, 46
Periplus of the Erythraean Sea, 11
Perlak, Aceh, 56
Persepolis, 56
Persia, 16, 56, 59
Persian art, 32
Persian Gulf, 16, 27, 56, 69
Persian language, 33
Peshawar, 51
Peshawer, 56
Peter Hopkirk, 44
Peter Turchin, 42
Petra, 25
Phaedra (Seneca), 12
Philip IV of France, 14
Pishan County, 53
Plague (disease), 2
Pliny the Elder, 12
Poduca, 56
Poland, 23
Polo, Marco, 45
Polychrome, 19
Polytimetus, 9

Poompuhar, 55, 56
Pope John XXII, 14
Pope Nicholas IV, 14
Poti, 47
Prehistoric, 59
Principate, 10
Procopius, 13
Protectorate General to Pacify the West, 19
Ptolemais Theron, 57
Ptolemy, 11, 56
Puer Hani and Yi Autonomous County, 63
Pujiang County, Sichuan, 64
Punjabi language, 33
Punjab region, 5
Pushkalavati, 51
Pyongyang, 54

Q36288, 46
Qazvin, 49
Qitai, 56
Quanzhou, 55
Quetta, 51

Rabban Bar Sauma, 14, 20
Rammed earth, 54
Raqqa, 48
Rasht, 49
Red Sea, 10, 16, 27, 57, 69
Rey, Iran, 49
Richard Foltz, 27, 41, 74
Roman Catholic Archdiocese of Beijing, 14
Roman commerce, 12
Roman currency, 8, 10
Roman economy, 3
Roman Egypt, 10
Roman emperor, 10
Roman Empire, 2, 3, 47
Roman glass, 40
Roman glassware, 10
Roman trade with India, 11
Rome, 55, 59
Round city of Baghdad, 18
Royal Road, 5, 71
Ruoqiang Town, 53

Sabzevar, 49
Safavid, 21
Salt, 61
Samanid Empire, 19
Samanids, 18
Samarkand, 20, 23, 50
Samarra, 48
Samatata, 51
Sampul tapestry, 6
Sana, 56
Sancai, 15, 38

Sangha, 28
Sanskrit, 33
Sarai (city), 18
Sarapion, 56
Sarmakhand, 18
Sarmatians, 9
Sarnath, 31
Sasanian Empire, 13
Sassanid Empire, 16
Saue, 56
Sayram (city), 50
Scythian, 4
Scythian art, 4
Scythians, 4
Seleucid, 9
Seleucid Empire, 6
Semylla, 56
Seneca the Younger, 12
Sennar, 56
Seres, 6, 9
Shaanxi, 4, 25, 59
Shahrisabz, 50
Shaki Caravanserai, 35
Shandan County, 54
Shanxi, 13
Sichuan, 26, 61, 62, 66
Sichuan-Tibet Railway, 63
Sijilmassa, 56
Silk, 2, 3, 19, 24, 26
Silk museums of Soufli, 13
Silk Road, **1**, 47, 48, 54, 59, 69
Silk Road Economic Belt, 23
Silk Roads, 47
Silk Road sites in India, 2
Silk Road UNESCO World Heritage Sites, 2, 32
Silla, 11, 12
Simplified Chinese characters, 61
Sinhalese language, 33
Sinitic, 16
Sino-Roman relations, 3
Smuggling of silkworm eggs into the Byzantine Empire, 13
Smyrna, 5
Sogdia, 3, 5, 13, 15, 19, 29, 38, 74
Sogdiana, 2, 6, 9, 10, 17, 29
Sogdians, 19
Solidus (coin), 14
Solkhat, 19
Somalia, 16, 25, 69
Somali language, 33
Somali people, 2
Somapura Mahavihara, 51
Sonargaon, 26, 51
Song dynasty, 13, 63
Sopatma, 56

South Asia, 61
South China Sea, 10, 27, 69
Southeast Asia, 2, 11, 27, 69
South East Asia, 57
Southern Europe, 2
Southern Silk Road: Through Khotan, 24
Southwest China, 61
Soviet Union, 3
Spice trade, 3, 27, 69
Spinel, 3
Spoke–hub distribution paradigm, 23
Sri Lanka, 10
Srivijaya, 56
Steatite, 4
Steppe Route, 3
Strabo, 6, 11
Strait of Malacca, 27, 69
Stuttgart, 4
Sudak, 55
Su Dingfang, 15
Suez, 55
Sui dynasty, 13
Suppara, 56
Susa, 5, 25
Suyab, 17
Suzhou District, 52
Sven Hedin, 3
Syncretic, 2
Syncretism, 6, 28
Syria, 48, 57
Syrian Desert, 25
Syrians, 2

Tabriz, 18, 21, 48
Tagalog language, 33
Ta-Hsia, 7
Tajikistan, 6, 50
Taklamakan, 59
Taklamakan Desert, 24, 25, 52, 53, 59
Talas River, 19
Talgar, 25, 59
Tamanrasset, 56
Tamil language, 33
Tang campaign against the Eastern Turks, 15
Tang campaign against the oasis states, 15
Tang dynasty, 13–15, 74
Tang Empire, 15
Tarakli, 47
Taraz, 17, 50
Tarim Basin, 7, 28, 29, 32
Tartus, 48
Tashkent, 22, 50
Taxila, 13, 51
Taxilla, 56
Tbilisi, 47
Tea brick, 63

Tea Horse Road, **61**
TEDx, 46
Tehran, 23, 49
Temple University Press, 73
Tenjiku, 9
Ter, Maharashtra, 56
Termez, 25
Thailand, 26
Thaton, 57
The Great Game: The Struggle for Empire in Central Asia, 44
The Travels of Marco Polo, 21
Three Kingdoms, 16
Tianquan, 65
Tian Shan, 25, 59
Tianshui, 54
Tianzhu County, Guizhou, 54
Tiberius, 10
Tibet, 26, 61, 66
Tibetan Empire, 19
Tibetan Pony, 63
Tigris, 5
Timur, 20, 50
Timurid Empire, 20
Tingis, 56
TLV mirror, 39
Tocharians, 29
Tom Engelhardt, 46
Trabzon, 21, 47
Trackway, 59
Trade, 10
Traditional Chinese characters, 61
Trang, Trang, 57
Trans-Eurasia Logistics, 22
Transoxiana, 7, 18
Treasure voyages, 22
Treaty of Aleppo, 21
Trier, 56
Turfan, 29, 74
Turkey, 5, 47
Turkic Khaganate, 13
Turkic peoples, 2
Turkish language, 33
Türkmenabat, 49
Turkmeni, 21
Turkmenistan, 49
Turkmen language, 33
Turpan, 25, 52, 59
Turpan water system, 52
Tus, Iran, 49
Twenty-Four Histories, 10, 14
Tymdis, 56
Tyre, Lebanon, 48

Uighur Empire, 17
Ulsan, 55

Umayyad, 18
Umayyad Caliphate, 19
UNESCO, 2, 69
United Nations, 32
United Nations Educational, Scientific and Cultural Organization, 32
University of Hawaii Press, 44
University of Massachusetts Press, 41
Urdu, 33
Urumqi, 6

Ürümqi, 22, 52

Uyghurs, 14
Uzbekistan, 19, 50
Uzbek language, 33

Valerie Hansen, 10
Varanasi, 51
Venice, 20, 55
Victor H. Mair, 44
Vietnam, 10
Vijaya (Champa), 55
Viktor Sarianidi, 43
Virgil, 12
Volga, 18

Wari-Bateshwar, 51
Wari-Bateshwar ruins, 26, 56
Warring States, 4
Warwick Ball, 3, 10, 71
Watchtower, 54
West Asia, 2
Western Asia, 47
Western culture, 1
Western Han dynasty, 26, 39
Western Regions, 15, 16, 19
Wikipedia:Citation needed, 3–5, 17, 19, 21, 25, 59
Wikt:maritime, 27
Wild silk, 4
William of Rubruck, 21
World Heritage Committee, 1
World Heritage Site, 1, 2, 69
World Tourism Organization, 32
Wusun, 7
Wuwei, Gansu, 54
W.W. Norton & Co, 45

Xian, 10, 25, 54, 59
Xiangtan, 22
Xi Jinping, 23
Xinjiang, 6, 8, 53
Xinjiang Province, 22
Xinru Liu, 27, 42, 45
Xiongnu, 7, 15, 28

Xuanzang, 29

Yaan, 61, 63, 66
Yangguan, 53
Yarkant County, 52, 53, 56
Yarkent County, 3
Yazd, 49
Yellow Sea, 27, 69
Yerevan, 48
Yuan dynasty, 13, 17
Yuezhi, 7
Yumen Pass, 52
Yunnan, 26, 61, 63, 66

Zafar, Yemen, 56
Zanjan, Iran, 49
Zeinodin Caravanserai, 37
Zhang Qian, 2, 7
Zhangye, 54
Zhang Yichao, 19
Zhejiang, 23
Zhou dynasty, 39
Zoroastrianism, 19, 27

89

www.ingramcontent.com/pod-product-compliance
Lightning Source LLC
LaVergne TN
LVHW041343080426
835512LV00006B/588

*9 7 8 9 3 5 2 9 7 9 6 5 3 *